DECISION TIME!

Better Decisions for a Better Life

By
Richard Davidson

"DECISION TIME! Better Decisions for a Better Life" by Richard
Davidson
ISBN 978-0-9829160-7-0
Second Edition, September, 2015 © 2015, Richard Davidson, All
rights reserved.
Published by RADMAR Publishing Group, P.O. Box 425,
Northbrook, IL 60065, U.S.A.

Manufactured in the United States of America.

This book is dedicated to the memory of my mother-in-law, Mildred Knol, who would length-ily vacillate between any two choices she faced, but who was loved by all who had the privilege of meeting her.

Cover art by Kim Nelson

I would like to acknowledge with great thanks the support of my wife Jean during the writing of this book and the time devoted by test readers of my manuscript and the constructive comments they generated.

Table of Contents

Chapter 1
Why You Are Where You Are

Where you are in life today is the result of the combination of all of the past decisions which you have made or which have been made for you in response to the various situations and events, both expected and unexpected, which have impacted your life. The decisions which you have not yet made and future decision-stimulating events will determine your continuing life circumstances. If you were able to review all of those past decisions, including the millions of small ones, and change a few here and there, you would end up in a greatly changed situation from the one you have now. This is why the making of decisions in life is so important. In fact, one could say that the story of your life is the record of all of those decisions and the events that stimulated them plus the results of those decisions. Because of this, it is very important to learn how to make good decisions and to evaluate their results in order to improve your future.

As an illustration of the effect a decision can make on the rest of your life, consider what Robert Frost wrote:

Two roads diverged in a wood, and I–
I took the one less traveled by,
And that has made all the difference.
The Road Not Taken [1916]

As indicated above, changes in past decisions—if possible—would lead to a different life situation than the one you have now. However, it is important to note that there is no way to know whether such changes would lead to a better or worse condition than your present one. It is even possible that over the course of time your changed situation would merge with your current path. This might be the case if there is fate or divine guidance in your life, but it might also be the result of basic personal inclinations shaping future decisions toward a personally desired result that may be either clearly known or buried in your subconscious.

The Robert Frost poem not only illustrates how a decision made today can affect the rest of your life, but it also shows that such a life-changing decision does not have to be a major one. A simple act of taking a different path at any crossroads along the course of your journey can have great and unforeseeable implications for you and for everyone else with whom you interact. Consider the wanderings of the Biblical Israelites led by Moses on their way to the Promised Land of Canaan from Egypt. They wandered in the desert for forty years before they arrived at their destination, while the straight-line path was less than two hundred miles. This book will help you to decide when changes in direction are desirable and advantageous for you.

In thinking back over past decisions and redirections in the course of your life, you should not engage in the practice of regretting either actual past decisions or those which should have been made but were left undone. We cannot do anything about the past except learn from it. The question should be "Where will our new decisions take us from here?" Shakespeare showed great insight when he said "what's past is prologue; what to come, in yours and my discharge." (*The Tempest,* Act II, Scene I) In this quotation he combines the belief that we must live in the present rather than the past, with an equally strong belief that you and I must take responsibility for the decisions that will lead us into the future. "Prologue" as used in the Shakespeare quotation does not mean that the past is unimportant to the present and future. On the contrary, the past trains and prepares us for each new step. Any two people in the same location, making the same decision at the same time, will be different in their preparation to carry out that decision because of the variations in their past training and experiences.

This book is essentially non-mathematical in nature. It has very little in common with texts analyzing statistically or mathematically modeled preferred outcomes in well-defined objective situations. Some mathematical terms and principles are used, but the basic theorem is that most decision situations are primarily subjective in nature and do not have a single well-defined preferred outcome. "Subjective" should not imply that there is no clear solution to a decision problem situation, but only that life is complicated and full of variables. You will learn principles that will assist you to determine the preferred decision in your subjective circumstances. It is very important for you to learn how to make good decisions because your decisions will make your future.

Chapter 2
Difficulties in Making Decisions

Some people seem to have an inherent inability to make decisions quickly.

They tend to fear the consequences of a bad decision to the point that they feel that any choice is bad. In some cases, this inability to decide is due to the emotional makeup of the individual, and in other cases it is due to that person having had bad experiences with past decisions. Hopefully, the tools presented in this book will simplify the decision-making process for such a person.

Even people who are not burdened with a tendency toward indecisiveness will frequently have problems making decisions. One reason for this may be that the arguments for and against a particular decision may be essentially of equal value. Many people do not want to make a decision unless the arguments on one side of the matter are overwhelming as compared to the arguments on the other side. Such people dread the necessity of making a decision in a "close call" situation. They are not well suited to being umpires, referees, or judges.

A third group of people having trouble with making decisions includes those individuals who have difficulty accepting responsibility. Such people want to go along with others in a group rather than making a decision that might change the direction of the group for better or for worse. An individual of this type does not even want to take responsibility for the correctness of a decision that will affect only him or her.

A fourth type of person having trouble making decisions is closely related to the previous type. This person has a very high respect for authority and wants the authority figure to make all the decisions. Such individuals are very dependent and would have difficulty living in isolation from others.

There are also some people who have difficulties with choices because they are like squirrels. Squirrels can make a quick decision when they are crossing a street and see a car approaching. Their problem is that it is always the same decision. Squirrels appear to be programmed to always retreat and go back to their starting side of the street whenever they see a car coming, even when they have plenty of time to complete their crossing. Similarly, there are people who will always go back to the *status quo* whenever they are about to make a decision, and they see complications coming. In both cases the decision- maker is too tentative to complete the action in the face of possible adversity. In the words of the song <u>Reviewing the Situation</u> from the musical, *Oliver*, they are telling themselves "...I think I'd better think it out again!"

Most people with decision difficulties belong to more than one of the foregoing groups. They are a combination of types, and may have additional factors that make decisions hard for them. Some people having none of the described traits may also have problems making decisions. In such cases the problem may be due to stress, the need to make many decisions simultaneously, or rapid variations in factors that are guides toward making wise choices. In a situation where many decisions need to be made, each decision may lead to changes in the factors which affect other decisions, and timing deadlines may make analysis even more difficult.

The point of this chapter is that there are many reasons why some people always tend to vacillate between alternatives when making decisions, and why everyone has such an indecision problem at some time. In the next chapter we will start to develop tools that will make decisions easier.

Chapter 3
The Subjective Nature of Decisions—Davidson's Doctrine

Real life situations are both complex and dynamic. They do not lend themselves to rigorous mathematical analysis because there are too many variable factors and because people think and react in unpredictable ways. In such an environment a particular stimulus or cause will not always produce the same effect. Thus, we have to describe our environment as requiring subjective analysis rather than objective analysis in order to reach most decisions. Further, we rarely have the luxury of making single infrequent decisions. While some decisions are of much higher importance than others we have to make them rapidly, and we have to consider the effects of our decisions on other people.

If almost all situations are subjective, that means that they appear differently to the various people who observe them. We have all read reports of multiple witnesses to an accident reporting significantly different versions of what happened and greatly different descriptions of the individuals and cars that were involved. Given such difference among the viewpoints of various people, how can we possibly reach decisions which will please everyone who is involved and which will appear to everyone to be correct? The initial answer is that we cannot and should not attempt to please everybody. The key to making a good decision is that it should be acceptable to you at the time you make it. If the result of that first decision is that it leads to new problems that must be resolved, remember that you can always make another decision at that point. Decisions are made to achieve a goal, but as decisions are made, new goals are developed, and new decisions are required. Decision-making is a never-ending process. Taking the first step by making the first decision overcomes the inertia of the *status quo* and starts the process rather than the event of decision-making. You make decisions of varying magnitude every day, and you will continue to do so throughout your life. The important thing is to understand the process of decision-making so that choices become routine steps along your journey through life rather than major obstacles.

You are the key to the process. The most important characteristic of any decision is that you should be comfortable with the outcomes that result from it. This must be true even though those outcomes will arise at some time in the future. How then can you make a wise decision now and feel comfortable with consequences that will not become evident until the future?

The answer to this question lies in an approach that I call <u>Davidson's Doctrine:</u>

Whenever you have to decide between two alternatives or among several alternatives, select one choice, and assume that you have already made that decision. Then look at your situation from the viewpoint of having already made the decision, and see whether you are comfortable with it and its probable resulting implications. Convert the assumed decision to an actual one only after you feel comfortable with all aspects of the assumed choice. If you find that you are not comfortable with the expected outcomes of the assumed decision, choose another alternative, and repeat the self-questioning to determine whether you are comfortable with the implications of that new decision.

In practice, this doctrine is easy to apply, but it requires some explanation and examples. Once you assume that you have made a particular decision, you move beyond it in order to find out whether you are comfortable with it. You should feel comfortable with your assumed decision by whatever criteria are important to you. Different people will have varying needs that they will want satisfied before proceeding to a real decision. You might ask yourself questions like:

- Now that I have (*assumed that I have*) made this decision, what do I have to do to follow up on it?
- How are my family and friends going to react to my decision?
- If this decision feels right to me, do I care what other people think and say about it?
- Am I ready to tell everyone about my decision?
- What is it going to cost in money, other resources, and intangible values to make this choice?
- What rewards can I expect from this decision?
- Am I ready to go beyond assuming that I have made this decision and actually make it?

You may find that it is helpful to go beyond the assumed decision and to take some minor actions based upon it to determine your level of comfort with that choice.

Example 1: When I first debated whether I should start my own business many years ago, I was working for Bell & Howell Company. I had become bothered by the amount of time that was spent in long meetings at this large company prior to making any significant decision. I was also discouraged by the attitude of many managers to avoid any step forward that might reflect poorly on the importance of their departments or their management style. They acted as though they worked for their departments rather than for the company as a whole.

At this time Bell & Howell Company was also having problems due to a product line that had old technology. I debated whether it was better to remain there and to hope for additional future advancement, or if it was better to go out on my own. As I mulled over my options, I looked at many of the small vendors we used and the people running those businesses, and I decided that I could run a business as well as they could. I didn't do anything that would change my status with the corporation, but I assumed that I was going to go out on my own. This assumption felt comfortable to me. While I continued to work for my employer, I took the preliminary steps of joining a workshop on starting a small business; working out a name, logo, and set of objectives for the business, and meeting with an attorney to begin the incorporation procedure. I also had some business cards and letterhead printed to give the new business a visible identity. None of these steps were costly, and they took me far enough down this new path to let me know that I was comfortable with it. I started to work on a first product in the evenings, and left Bell & Howell only after I felt that the product would be viable when completed, but before it was developed to the point where they might assert a claim on it. My new company was incorporated on April 30th, and I resigned from Bell & Howell on June 1st of that year.

Example 2: The first car I owned was a 1956 Chevy Bel Air convertible.

I loved that car, and in recent years I have repeatedly thought that I would buy one on the classic car market if I could get one. I made the assumption that I had decided to buy one, and followed up this assumption by looking for similar cars at antique car shows and museums. After a period of this assumed shopping, I decided that I was not comfortable with the prospect of buying that car, and I rid myself of that temptation permanently. I had realized that I did not have the large amount of money that I would have needed to spend on it; I did not have a good place to keep it; and I was quite satisfied to just see similar cars occasionally at car shows and museums. I had also developed a recurring dream that I had purchased my car and that it had been stolen. After the ninth or tenth time of dreaming that I had lost my prized possession to a thief, I decided that I was not destined to own that classic car. As a much less costly alternative, I purchased an original repair manual for the car online; had my picture taken next to a museum car; and surrounded myself with miniature models of it. My assumed decision had taken me through the process and relieved me of my unsatisfied desire.

Whether the result of the assumed decision is to make it a permanent choice or to turn to an alternative action, you will learn something about yourself during the process, and it won't cost you anything significant to find out whether you are comfortable with the assumed decision. This approach gives you the opportunity to learn from your mistakes before you make them. In a sense it is like seeing into the future or having 20-20 foresight. In some cases the consequences of an assumed decision that you avoid by realizing your discomfort may be very significant, as in the case of avoiding a marriage to an incompatible spouse or of making an impractical or unethical business move. When you do decide to proceed with the assumed decision, you have already rehearsed it and reviewed its various implications, so the actual implementation of the decision will be easier for you than if you were acting on a snap judgement. When you go through the assumed decision process you are effectively going through a procedure to formalize the old adage of sleeping on a problem before taking action to resolve it.

Learning from assumed decisions can also be valuable when minor choices are required. For example, if you tell yourself that you would like to enter a long-distance race and start practicing in the rigorous way which would be required, you will soon discover whether or not you are comfortable with the burden of regular training. The important point is that you will learn your degree of comfort with the decision without having made a formal commitment to the race organization or to your friends and family. Another benefit of assuming that you have made a decision before you actually make it is that you will have time to consider the effects of that decision on others before it becomes a commitment. This makes the assumed decision a diplomatically sound and considerate process. You have the opportunity to learn whether you are comfortable with it before you potentially hurt someone else's feelings or embarrass yourself.

Applying Davidson's Doctrine:

Assume that you have made a decision to run for public office. What preliminary steps would you take to decide whether you would be comfortable with this decision? Are you comfortable with the impact that this decision would have on those with whom you have relationships? Does the effort required feel worthwhile in order to achieve your objective? How would you go about raising money and determining how much money you would need? How would you react if your opponent used dirty campaign tactics against you? Would you feel comfortable serving in that office if you were elected? What would be the impact of that election on your family, friends, and business activities? How would you feel if you lost the election?—You should be able to get a feeling for the steps involved in the assumed decision process from this example. Without getting anyone else prematurely involved, you should soon know whether you are comfortable with this choice.

Chapter 4
Corollaries to Davidson's Doctrine

Corollary One: To determine your best comfort level in a given decision situation, include the option of making no decision at all.

Some people feel that they have to always be in control of a situation and that such control requires a continuous stream of decisions. In many situations the best decision is to just allow things to happen without any controlling decision on your part.

Consider the famous "Prayer of Serenity" of St. Francis of Assisi:

God, grant me the serenity to accept the things I cannot change; the courage to change the things I can; and the wisdom to know the difference.

This prayer has always bothered me, because it implies that if you *can* change something, you *should*. That is not always the case. There are many times when change is possible but not desirable. The Declaration of Independence emphasizes the goals of "Life, Liberty, and the Pursuit of Happiness". Pursuing happiness is a dynamic process, but what about statically accepting happiness when you reach a reasonable approximation of that goal? The old army adage says, "If it ain't broke, don't fix it!" Sometimes a decision to make a change is not necessary. Go back to seeing if you are more comfortable with remaining where you are rather than with making a decision in favor of change. This, by the way, is the argument that political incumbents always make during an election campaign.

When you are sailing a small boat, and the wind suddenly shifts direction so that the sail wants to swing in a different direction, you can get in serious trouble and even capsize if you take action to fight against the sudden wind shift. The safest and easiest thing to do is simply to slack off on all the lines and let the sail spill its air. This gets you to a static but stable situation. Once you are stable, you can take time to determine what you should do to take advantage of the new wind instead of fighting it.

There have been a number of studies made to determine the best investment strategy in the stock market. Many of these have concluded that regularly periodic purchasing of stocks to be held for long-term investment is a better strategy than making numerous short-term changes in your portfolio in response to the dynamics of the market. This long-term approach also saves you lots of money in transaction fees and capital gains taxes.

Other situations where the best decision (Yes, this is also a decision.) is to make no decision include cases where you genuinely like the *status quo* and cases where the cost (in money, prestige, difficulty, etc.) of making a decision is very large. Human inertia ("Don't rock the boat!") is an important attitudinal factor leading to a "no decision" situation.

Corollary Two: Stick with a new decision for a reasonable period of time unless conditions change.

Making a decision changes the dynamics of your situation in life. It is like throwing a stone into a placid lake and watching the rings of wavelets move radially outward from the point of the stone's splash. If you have gone through the assumed decision process and have found advance comfort with the decision to throw that stone, there is no need to worry about the result unless you receive new relevant information. The lake will not become placid while you continue to throw new stones. After the dynamic action of making a decision, be deliberate about your next step, and let the decision lead to a new stable situation from which point you are free to determine your next appropriate step.

There's an Old Irish saying that goes something like this:

You either have good health or bad health.

If you have good health, there's no need to worry.

If you have bad health,

You will either get better or worse.

If you get better, there's no need to worry.

If you get worse,

You will either live or die.

If you live, there's no need to worry.

If you die,

You will either go to heaven or hell.

If you go to heaven, there's no need to worry.

If you go to hell,

You will meet all of your old friends and relatives there.

So, why worry?

Worrying never solves anything. Worrying only makes it difficult to make and evaluate your next assumed decision.

Another aspect of being deliberate about decisions is that you should avoid being rushed into your next decision by someone trying to apply coercion or high-pressure sales techniques. Unless your decision is required for the world or someone's life not to end immediately, you should stall or consult with others until you have thought the matter through to the point of being comfortable with your decision. The very existence of high-pressure sales tactics is usually a sign that the items or services being sold do not sell easily. I personally take high-pressure sales methods as a red flag signal to proceed with extreme caution.

In scientific analysis of the way to improve any situation, the key principle is to change only one variable at a time and to determine the results of changing that variable before changing anything else. Changing multiple variables simultaneously guarantees that the effect you observe will not be attributable to a single identifiable cause. Similarly, worrying introduces additional variables into your subjective decision making. All of those "What ifs?" that result from worrying will keep you from finding your comfort level with a new assumed decision or will make it difficult to evaluate the results of a decision you have recently made. Worrying accomplishes nothing, and it is the enemy of the stable state that will assist you in making future decisions.

Corollary Three: In most subjective life situations, there is more than one "right" decision.

Unlike the Ten Commandments, decisions you make are not carved in stone and destined to remain unchanged forever. There is always the option of making another decision to work toward undoing any unwanted effect. Further, most life decisions are more like answering an essay question on a test rather than a "True-False" or even a multiple-choice type. Because most subjective decisions involve many factors there are almost always multiple decisions that will be acceptable at least for the short term. This will be the situation especially when you have incomplete knowledge of all circumstances. As you get more knowledge, you can review your first choice to see whether you are still comfortable with it. One value of Davidson's Doctrine is that by using it to evaluate the comfort level of an assumed decision, you can readily find an <u>acceptable </u> decision. More than one such <u>acceptable </u> decision may exist, but at least you will know that you have found one of them. It would be possible to assume several alternate decisions to determine whether you are comfortable with them, but in most cases this is not recommended, because due to their subjective nature, it might be difficult to evaluate the relative comfort levels of those several acceptable decisions. Additional techniques will be discussed in Chapter 11 to handle this type of analysis.

One situation having no single correct choice occurs when you are looking at a menu in a good restaurant that prepares many things well. You can use the assumed decision process to eliminate one or more of the tempting choices, but the good news is that if the restaurant is good enough, any one of the remaining selections will be good.

The fact that more than one acceptable decision usually exists is the key to the negotiation process. Whether the context is diplomacy, business contracts, or a family planning their Thanksgiving dinner, the existence of multiple acceptable decisions will allow for the possibility that all parties to the negotiation can be satisfied. This is the goal that should always be sought. We will discuss negotiations in more detail later.

Corollary Four: Even a bad decision has worth.

Because we deal with complex situations on a regular basis, we will occasionally make a really bad decision. Remember that in most such cases, a bad decision can be offset by a subsequent better decision. It may take several such better decisions to completely cancel the damage of the bad choice, but that is how we learn and grow. For example, an early decision to smoke and the resulting addiction to smoking can be reversed by medication, willpower, and determination over a period of time but several decisions to quit may be required before success is achieved. Smoking is a bad decision, but we can learn from it that our body is not indestructible and that it is important to consider effects on our health when making a choice.

We learn more from the process of recovering from a bad decision than we do from a prolonged series of good decisions. For example, a sports team that has been very successful may listen to the press and their fans and become convinced that they are unbeatable. They may decide that their next opponent is not serious competition and may be very surprised when they lose badly. This loss may do more to let the team understand where they need to improve than a whole series of victories over weaker teams. In addition, such a loss will be a valuable lesson in humility and the importance of objective self-evaluation.

In general we learn more from adversity than from success. We always try to avoid adversity, but everyone encounters it sometime. The important thing is to be open to the possibility of learning from the results of a bad decision. It is not useful to try to assign blame when a bad decision has been made. Instead, take the approach of saying, "Well, here is the current situation. What should I do to move on to a better one from where I am now?" You can't avoid problems altogether; you have to identify and overcome them by good future choices. You also should remember the bad decisions and their consequences so that you won't repeat your mistakes in the future.

Chapter 5
Sequences of Decisions

When you are doing graphical plotting of distances on a map, the sequence of your steps is not important. The sequence: one mile (or kilometer) East, two North, three West, four South produces exactly the same resulting location as the alternate sequence: four South, three West, one East, two North. This result is very objective and mathematically elegant when you are plotting distances on a map or a piece of graph paper. However, it doesn't work as well in the real world.

Even if you are making a simple sequence of decisions in driving your car across local terrain, you will find that the mapping example doesn't accurately apply.

- A mile (kilometer) you drive may be shorter than a mile (kilometer) as represented on the map because of hills, valleys, and curves in the road.

• Because all roads are different, one mile (kilometer) going North, East, West, and South will each be different due to variations in terrain and road curviness and hence will correspond to different distances on the map. For this reason alone, you would end up at different locations depending on the sequences of distances that you took.

• Whether you are in an urban or rural area, you may find that it is impossible to drive any sequence of four one-mile (kilometer) distances in the four primary compass directions. There may be no road junctions at the desired turn location; there may be no roads going in the desired direction; or there may be major obstacles in the way. On the latter point, consider the fact that from where I sit writing, driving a significant distance east would have my car in Lake Michigan.

The point of the foregoing exercise is to emphasize that objective mathematical decision exercises are based on approximations to the real world. In order to work with a manageable number of variables mathematicians often simplify the real world when they try to make calculated decisions. Alternately, they use statistics and probabilities to select decisions based on large numbers of events that have actually happened. The techniques presented in this book will help an individual make personal or business decisions in a subjective situation without having to gather any information that is not already known. These techniques are simple; yet they allow for the complexities and surprises of life.

The following is a more obvious illustration of the importance of the sequence of the decisions you make. To decide to: (Go to college; start a career; get married; have children.) will get you into an entirely different life situation than if you decide to: (Have children; start a career; get married; go to college.) The more traditional former path is likely to be less stressful than the latter path. The unconventional latter sequence would likely require more creativity in overcoming obstacles along the way.

Sequences of decisions in life are important not only in determining where you will end up, but also in determining the path you take to get there. The old Confucian saying: "A journey of a thousand miles starts with a single step." is true, but the sequence of decisions you make beyond that first step will determine what you see along the way. Frequently, the path you take will be more meaningful and will contribute more to your wellbeing or lack of it than will be the reaching of your eventual destination. Further, since we all have limited lifetimes, we consciously and subconsciously strive to prolong the path that is our life and to make it as interesting as possible.

Chapter 6
The Concept of Personal Logic

We each approach any situation with our own set of personal traits and history. No two people are alike. This point was made clear to me some years ago when I attended a multi-church gathering where a speaker made the statement that we are each "a unique unrepeatable miracle of God". Regardless of your religion or lack of it, I hope that you will agree with the uniqueness aspect of this statement. Because we are unique, it is unreasonable to assume that in a particular situation we would all logically do the same thing or have identical qualifications.

If you are at a beach, and a swimmer calls for help, it is logical that the lifeguard or a person who is a strong swimmer should go to that person's aid rather than a kind-hearted individual who does not know how to swim. When the rescued person turns out to speak only Spanish, it is logical to look for a Spanish speaking individual to try to find out what happened to the swimmer. If the swimmer needs medical attention it is logical to call 911 rather than to have someone without medical knowledge give him an aspirin.

We each have our own set of experiences, capabilities, and bodies of knowledge that determine the personal logic of our doing a certain task or taking on a certain responsibility. The assignment decision that will usually result in the best comfort level for all in a given situation is that the best-prepared individual should take the responsibility. In some cases the logic of available capabilities may say that it is best for a team of individuals to tackle a specific task when no one person is well suited to do so.

In the beach example cited above, note the dynamic nature of personal logic in a situation. The lifeguard may have been the best rescuer, but if he or she did not have knowledge of Spanish, the lifeguard was not the appropriate person for the next step, the interview. The best interviewer probably did not have the medical knowledge required for further treatment of the rescued swimmer, so calling 911 was the appropriate decision.

Personal logic is useful when you are deciding whether to volunteer for a particular task or whether a supervisor should select you. In work or political situations the decision-maker is frequently someone in a higher authority position, and the choice may not be based on logic but on rewarding past behavior or on developing a sense of future obligation. When someone who is unsuitable for the task is selected, it becomes an awkward and inefficient situation. Such cases tend to give a sense of comfort to no one except the authority figure, and they generate repressed feelings among the various staff members that can cause problems later.

Personal logic may also be useful to you when you are trying to decide whether to learn a new skill or to take on a job you have never done before. Your personal knowledge of your history and skills may tell you that it is logical to add to your skills in an area of weakness. Even though you may decide to do something for which you are not well prepared, you may feel comfortable with the decision because you know that you will be adding to your skills and possibilities for the future. If you are confident by nature, you may find it worthwhile to say "Yes!" to every new challenge or job on the assumption that you will be able to learn how to do it or will be able to find resources from others to do it. This has always been Standard Operating Procedure in my company, and it has been amazing how readily we have developed the skills and resources to handle new jobs that we had never previously considered or tried. Many small businesses have become large businesses by using this strategy.

Even if you have had a series of failures in the past, personal logic may tell you to accept new challenges in the hope of learning from your failures and achieving successes. In high school I had a friend who was not very well known or popular. Long before high school graduation he had decided that when he went to college, he would take advantage of the fact that everyone would be equally unknown to each other, and he would run for freshman class president. He felt that this action would give him a new chance at popularity whether he won the election or not. Would such an approach appeal to you? If you are pessimistic you might feel that you would fail again, but if you are optimistic you might feel that you would be overdue for a success. Use the principle of assuming that you have already accepted the challenge, and see whether you become comfortable with that outlook before you make your final decision.

Another aspect of personal logic that is worth discussing relates to the difference between actual and apparent skills of an individual. If a supervisor is selecting someone for a task, he or she will select that person based on known skills. If you have skills that are not known to the supervisor and want the assignment, make your capabilities known, either verbally or by drawing the supervisor's attention to similar tasks that you have already performed well. As an example, while I was in college, I was in charge of organizing the concert tour for the Glee Club and also for organizing guest artist concerts on campus by classical artists as well as by popular performers such as Ella Fitzgerald and Tom Lehrer. When I later was a young engineer with an aerospace contractor, I used my concert management background to convince them that I should be Project Manager on a new contract effort.

Chapter 7
Setting Priorities

At any given time there are multiple decisions and tasks that are facing you, whether you are considering business or personal matters, or a combination of the two. You will feel much less pressure in making such decisions if you set priorities for yourself. It is relatively easy to set priorities, and the more you get used to doing it, the easier it will become. The basic principle is to compare any two tasks in order to determine whether it is more important to do the first task or the second one. If you have a large set of tasks or decisions to make, simply compare each additional item beyond the first two with each of those to which you have already assigned a relative priority. For instance, if you have already decided that it is more important to <u>Get car repaired</u> than to <u>Go to dentist</u>, compare the importance of each of those items with a third item such as <u>Pack for business trip</u>. Fourth and fifth items such as <u>Pay bills</u> and <u>Deposit paycheck</u> could be considered in the same way. This technique can be expanded to any number of items, but for the set of tasks we have described, you might end up with a priority list that looks like:

1. Get car repaired
2. Pay bills.
3. Go to dentist.
4. Pack for business trip.
5. Deposit paycheck

This kind of list makes decisions much easier to accomplish. You just have to make your decisions and perform your tasks in the sequence of your priority list. If this were a simple and static world this set of priorities would rule your day's activities. Unfortunately, our world is complex, and it is necessary both to allow for new or cancelled activities and to handle shifts in the priority of items that are already on your list. As an example, if you had to cancel the business trip in favor of finishing a report, and if you suddenly developed a bad toothache, the list might change to:

1. Go to dentist.
2. Finish report.
3. Pay bills
4. Get car repaired.
5. Deposit paycheck

If the dentist required immediate payment for his services, the list might become:
1. Deposit paycheck.
2. Go to dentist
3. Finish report.
4. Get car repaired.
5. Pay bills.

If the bills were already past due, the list might become:
1. Deposit paycheck
2. Go to dentist.
3. Pay bills.
4. Finish report.
5. Get car repaired.

You can see in these examples that the original top priority, Get car repaired is now in last place on the list because the business trip has been cancelled. Similarly, the original last place item, Deposit paycheck is now in first place because of the need to pay the dentist and the past due bills. In the middle of the list you probably would be having an internal debate over whether it was more important to pay the bills or finish the business report.
The points that I want to emphasize are:
- The setting of priorities is a great tool for deciding the sequence in which multiple decisions should be made or multiple tasks should be done.
- Priorities have to be changed continuously as items to be done are added to the list or subtracted from it.

- Priorities have to be changed as items in the list become more or less important due to events you cannot foresee.
- Priorities compete with one another. There may be valid arguments for several items to be top priority.
- As in the case of the business trip that was cancelled in favor of completing the report, you cannot set priorities in isolation from the rest of the world. The priorities that you set may not match those of your business associates, spouse, or negotiation adversary. They even have to be examined to determine whether they are appropriate in relationship to the moves of the stock market, international conflicts, and natural disasters.
- Priority setting for lower level tasks may be avoided if they are part of a normal routine. This simplifies many minor decisions; however, even routines should be reviewed periodically to determine whether they are still appropriate or efficient. The business or government equivalent of a routine for daily activities may take the form of a Procedures Manual.
- At different times the relative value of the rating scales may change. Sometimes you will want to maximize the cash value of the alternate tasks. At other times you may set priorities in order to minimize the time required for the tasks. There may also be times when priorities are set based on a reward system such as Frequent Flyer miles, tax deductions, or (for those who

<u>are old enough to remember them)</u> Green Stamps.

The conscious or subconscious setting of priorities is not only a valuable tool, but it is <u>required</u> when decisions have to be made involving a large number of competing or essentially simultaneous activities. Elaborate mathematical procedures such as linear programming have been developed to assist in such situations, but they are only as good as the subjective input to the programmer regarding the relative values and difficulties of all of the tasks. Without wisdom in setting the task characteristics, the mathematical procedures produce apparently sophisticated but illogical results. The PERT (Program Evaluation and Review Technique) network tool was developed by the U.S. Navy to determine the critical path of tasks required for completion of a complex project in the minimum amount of time. In this technique the critical path is identified as that set of interconnected sequential activities in the planning network that take the longest time. The objective is to reduce the time of tasks on the critical path because reducing the time of those tasks reduces the time to finish the whole project. The PERT Network project control system is only as good as the detailed input regarding the time required for each and every task and the nature of the interrelationships among all of those tasks. These mathematical tools extend the subjective setting of priorities to complex project situations, but they are no better than the assumptions and estimates that are used for their input data.

Chapter 8
Negotiation and Diplomacy

Some of the most intense forums requiring the making of a large number of decisions are those involving negotiation and diplomacy. These more formal decision-making gatherings are particularly well suited to the use of Davidson's Doctrine. When you assume that you have already made a particular decision, you will find it easier to predict what reaction your negotiation opponent will take when he or she reacts to your assumed decision. Negotiations are basically adversarial procedures, and the job of the negotiator or negotiating team is to reach decisions with which both sides can feel comfortable. This is the compromise process. Negotiated solutions are only possible when both sides acknowledge the possibility of compromise. When one or both sides are completely unwilling to accept changes from their original positions, no solution is possible. In multilateral negotiations the goal is for all parties to feel comfortable with the final outcome. The best way to achieve this balance is to be sure that all parties come away from the negotiations feeling that they have gained more than they have lost.

The first principle of negotiation is that you must be sensitive to the needs of others when you set priorities for what you hope to accomplish. If all parties have the same list of priorities, then it is unlikely that the negotiations will be successful. However, it is usually the case that there will be differences in the priority lists for the two or more parties to the negotiations. This will allow a final outcome where more than one party comes away from the process having satisfied his top priority goal. By being sensitive to the desires of others, you can set your priorities into a structure that makes negotiation success more likely.

The second principle of negotiation is that you must make it very clear to your opponent which are your top priorities and how determined you are to achieve them. It is a fact of human nature that if you are able to reach a decision that gains your top priority objective too easily, you will feel that you could have negotiated an even better outcome. This is true whether you are setting the price for the purchase of a used car or if you are involved in a complex labor contract negotiation. For this reason, most negotiations will and should start out with a firm statement of your goals. These goals should be reiterated and should seem to be inflexible for as long as possible. There is acting involved in such posturing, but the objective is to find out which party most desires a positive outcome to the negotiations. That party will usually show the first sign of flexibility. If no such flexibility is seen on either side, progress may have to be made as the result of setting a deadline or introducing a third party to mediate the process. A final alternative to inflexibility is to walk away from the negotiation process. If and only if your opponent believes that you are truly willing to stop the process, moving to end the negotiations may actually introduce flexibility from your adversary and stimulate the process toward success.

The third principle of negotiation is that although you frequently will have to resolve conflicts by giving in to someone else's viewpoint, you should always try to get something back in return for your willingness to see things their way. This is usually an acceptable and expected trade procedure. Even when there may not be an item on the table that your opponent is willing to give up in exchange for your flexibility, you may be able to gain something by proposing that he or she commit to a future benefit for you. This is why so many sports team trade negotiations end up including "a player to be named later" or a future draft choice. It is easier to reach agreement in this way because neither party knows the true value of a future benefit.

The fourth principle of negotiation is that decisions proceed from the bottom to the top. For this reason, it may be useful to have some low priority points on which you are willing to give in to your opponent's viewpoint. They may mean little to you, but after you have relinquished something, it is reasonable for you to expect your adversary to offer you something in return. Not only are smaller points agreed before larger points, but also in formal team negotiations there is a "pecking order" for personnel on the two sides.

The fifth principle of negotiation is that when you are not sure what to decide on a particular point, the best tactic is to add something to the discussion which "puts the ball in the other party's court" and gives your opponent responsibility for the next decision. This approach gives you more time to reach the decision that was facing you, and it may also give you new and valuable information from your opponent's response on the new matter.

The sixth principle of negotiation is that you can't please or accommodate everyone. You will definitely have to say *No* in many situations, and you will have to be firm about it. The word *No* has great value in that it can be used to reverse or slow down the momentum of a negotiation. You may be willing to concede additional points to your adversary, but judicious use of the word *No* will help you to gain return concessions and will help you to minimize those items on which you have to yield. It also helps to create an image of you as a tough negotiator, and in negotiations *image* is very important.

The seventh principle of negotiation is that the party with the greatest detailed knowledge of the matters being discussed has a great advantage. If you have all the details immediately available while your adversary has to repeatedly call for assistance from others or request a break in the process to obtain more information, you are negotiating from strength while the other party is negotiating from weakness. It is very important that you have done your homework before the meetings even start.

I was once involved in a negotiation to resolve a contract dispute between Bell & Howell Company and the U.S. government. Bell & Howell owned a film production company, Wilding Studios, which had worked with NASA to develop training materials for the early astronauts. The astronauts had to be able to fly a three-orbit mission around the Earth in a space capsule simulator, and they had to be able to look out the window of the simulator and see the terrain over which they were passing. The problem was that no one had previously flown such a mission, so the trainers had to show the astronauts something that no one had ever seen before. Wilding's job was to generate the orbital views of the Earth that did not yet exist. In order to do this they had constructed a very accurate model of the Earth's surface in a huge room. They then had precisely moved a special camera above the model to generate a continuous image of what an astronaut would see during his first three orbits of the Earth. The unique films they generated were approximately six inches wide.

The government's purchasing people claimed that the work had not been fully completed to their satisfaction, and they did not want to make the final payment that Wilding felt was due. A negotiation to resolve the issue was set up in a small federal building in Binghamton, New York. Each side had a team for the negotiation. An outside consultant who specialized in negotiations led our team. The Contract Administrator led the government team that also included accounting and training people from NASA. In addition to the Wilding people who had worked on the project and the consultant, our team had me as a technical consultant from Bell & Howell's Research and Development Department and my boss who was a Vice President and the foremost technology person in the company. The consultant had wanted the two of us included to give more status to our team and to show that the company felt that the resolution of the contract dispute was very important.

On the day before the negotiations were to start, we met with the consultant. He described in detail the probable stages in the negotiations, and he assigned specific roles to each member of the team. These role descriptions were very valuable because we entered the negotiations knowing exactly what would be expected of us as the negotiations progressed from stage to stage.

The negotiations started out with discussions by both full teams in a getting-to-know-you meeting across from each other at the usual gray steel, government-standard conference table in a drab bare-walled room. This phase went smoothly and was mostly intended to show that both sides were represented by appropriate people to discuss the issues. Then, after a short break, we went through a stage where our side was represented by the consultant and by the people who had directly worked on the project. My boss and I were not included in these discussions.

During that lengthy stage, the government kept insisting that we had not completed our tasks under the contract while we kept insisting that all work had been done properly but that the government agency had chosen to reject the finished product in order to avoid its financial obligations. After these talks had reached a stalemate (which was intentional per the planning of our consultant), they were reorganized as a technical working group. For this phase, the Contract Administrator and our consultant dropped out, leaving the people from Wilding who had worked on the project opposite the contract support staff for NASA. At this point I joined the talks as the unbiased technical "expert" from Bell & Howell rather than from Wilding Studios.

In this configuration we were free to go over the details of what had been done in comparison with the details of what the contract demanded. Where there was a conflict, I would step in as a third party to give my opinion on the technical merits of the work that had been done. I was careful to remain objective, and on some points I sided with the agency representatives. By working through the process item by item, examining both the contract and the finished training transparency film, we were able to agree that Wilding had substantially performed in compliance with the requirements except for a few specific details. We also confirmed the accuracy of the view that the astronaut would see during his simulated three orbits of the Earth.

These decisions triggered a new phase of the negotiation during which the Contract Administrator met with our consultant and my boss to reach a settlement of the remaining outstanding issues. Because of the detailed analysis that had been made at the technical level and because of informal conversations that had occurred at the administrative level during the technical discussions, a settlement agreement was readily formulated. It was signed by the Contract Administrator for the government and by my boss as a Vice President for the company. The important point illustrated here is that both sides expected a compromise to be reached and made sure that they were each represented by someone who had the authority to sign off on the final agreement without additional delay. Delays only open the door for more disagreements to arise. The government achieved its goal of showing that contractors have to strictly follow the details of each contract, and Wilding received virtually all the money that it was due.

During the negotiations described above, I served as an intermediary between the company technical people and the agency contract staff even though I was an employee of a different part of the company. This was not a formally arranged function such as a mediator, but a practical one. It was acceptable to the government people because we had demonstrated by our behavior and the quality of our staff that we were negotiating in good faith. It also made up for the fact that the government had not brought a technically trained person on their team.

It is very important to the success of any negotiation process that the adversarial teams respect each other. If there is not enough trust between the parties, one or more members may have to be changed in order to avoid a failure of the process. Where there are repeated negotiations between parties over a period of time, consistent good faith bargaining can lead to the buildup of "trust capital" which can be drawn upon at times to sway a stubborn negotiation in your favor.

Infrequently, it may be necessary to step out of character and use a climactic confrontation to reach a successful settlement of a negotiation. This is only possible when one side is negotiating in good faith, and the other is trying to bully and con their way to an advantageous resolution of the conflict. Such a standoff may only be resolved by the use of confrontation by the good faith team to define the limits and boundaries of negotiation tactics. In this situation a determined good faith team will almost always have the advantage because the belligerent team has already assumed that they will not encounter significant resistance, and they have wasted the value of climactic conflict by being continuously belligerent. Climactic conflict only works when it is a surprise tactic from a normally benign opponent.

This confrontation tactic is also useful in informal settings when someone has been continuously berating you because you don't agree with their opinion or their interpretation of proper organizational procedures. Some individuals will loudly push their viewpoint ceaselessly if they don't encounter open resistance. Your sudden transformation from a docile listener to an emphatic adversary will usually win your point in the debate and frequently will convert your opponent into an associate who now respects the strength of your opinions.

Diplomacy, whether interpersonal or international, uses the process of negotiation to reach decisions that are hopefully satisfactory to all parties through techniques that try to minimize any "bad aftertaste" from the resulting decisions. President John F. Kennedy voiced the key to diplomacy when he stated that we should always expect other countries to act in their own "enlightened self-interest" during negotiations. In diplomacy, politeness and protocols for "correct" behavior become very important. Diplomatic negotiations are built on the premise that the parties will have a long-term relationship and that no single negotiation outcome can be allowed to be so damaging to one party that future relationships are irreparably harmed. For example, if you are having an argument with your spouse, you should always remain conscious of the fact that your relationship is more important than the outcome of the debate. People have long memories, and things said during the passion of an argument can have bad implications for years, or even destroy the relationship altogether. The same is true for arguments between countries.

The polite formalities of diplomacy are there to give all parties the aura of mutual respect, and extreme efforts are made to give everyone the feeling that their party achieved something through the process. Such achievements may be tangible or intangible. In some international negotiations the objective of a country may be economic aid. However, in others formal recognition of a new government or of the merits of their current activities may be even more important.

These principles of diplomacy are useful in applying Davidson's Doctrine to your everyday decisions. When you assume that you have already made a required decision be sure to consider the impact of that decision on your relationships with all persons who might be involved. If your decision might adversely affect an important ongoing relationship, you may want to modify it.

Chapter 9
Dynamics of Decisions

There is no such thing as a decision that will be the best one forever. Some will be acceptable for a long time, but the logic that made them suitable for you when made will not apply indefinitely. Additional value for that decision will be required to keep it valid. This is one of the secrets of a long and happy marriage. People get married for relatively simple reasons. People stay married because they learn more and more about each other and share a multitude of experiences. As their interdependence matures, they appreciate each other more, and they subconsciously decide that it is much more mutually beneficial to maintain the relationship than to end it. In most cases the couple never even realizes that such a decision has been made or even considered.

Situations continuously change, and all decisions have to be open to review for possible change or modification. No decision can be made in isolation. By the time you have made one decision, the circumstances that triggered it have changed. Someone once said that there is nothing constant in life except change. This is why decisions are required on a continuous basis. Each choice affects others who make their choices, and you have to respond to them and to the changing environment in which you live. Nobody knows the future, but the more you learn to feel comfortable with the decision process, the better prepared you will be for that unknown future into which you are creeping. As indicated earlier, at each choice point you should assume that you have already made the decision and think through the implications of that decision to determine whether you will feel comfortable with it. At that point you can knowledgeably make the decision definite, but you should follow it up by analyzing the impact of that choice on yourself and others. You may find that changes either initiated by your decision or independently arising will require that you soon make an additional follow-up decision. Decision-making is a continuous process, and you may find that changes in one sector of your life will affect others in a major way. Some new decisions will be minor adjustments and will not affect others very much. However, when you make a major change in the style or direction of your life, you can expect decisions by others in response to it. Your life's direction might be varied due to major changes in

health, relationships, economic/business situations, legal requirements, or the abrupt and
unanticipated impact of natural and man-made
disasters.

Chapter 10
Decisions in Games

One area of life that emphasizes and exalts the need to make a continuous series of dynamic decisions in response to those made by others is the playing of games. The decision-making skills learned in such activities are so valuable that specialized games are becoming a standard device for teaching complex materials, especially now that computers are widely available to almost everyone. We participate in both formal and informal games, the winner of which is usually determined by a combination of probabilities, talent, luck, and the quality of decisions that are made.

The simplest game is probably flipping a coin. Given enough flips and a standard coin, the probability of the coin landing heads up will be very close to 50%. In this game there are very few decisions to be made because the results depend on probabilities that are not likely to change. The probability may seem different over a small number of flips when a series of heads (or tails) is encountered. When you run into such a series, you may decide that it will continue to occur, or you may decide that the opposite side of the coin is now overdue to come up.

The same probability question may arise in a very complex game. During the early days of the Illinois Lottery, I worked with someone who had developed a computer program to chart the results of the lottery. The results shown by that program were very interesting. They indicated that over the early course of the lottery certain numbers had come up much more frequently than others, even though, in theory, all of the numbered balls were equally likely to come up. The problem with this computer program was that it left you in the same position as with the small number of coin flips discussed above. You had more information than people who did not use the computer program, but you didn't know whether to bet that a number that had come up frequently was likely to continue to come up, or was overdue to fail to come up.

There are some games and situations where a different probability system, Bayesian probabilities, can help you to make a decision. Bayesian probabilities are also called "Personal Probabilities". As in the case of Personal Logic, discussed in Chapter 4, Bayesian Probabilities depend on your existing knowledge when you have to make a decision. Take the simple hand game of Paper, Rock, and Scissors wherein:

- Paper (hand out flat) wins against a rock because it can wrap it, but loses to a pair of scissors because scissors can cut the paper.
- A rock (hand out in a fist) beats the scissors because the scissors would break in trying to cut the rock, but loses to the paper
- The scissors (two fingers out in a "V") beats the paper, but loses to the rock as previously indicated.

In terms of standard probabilities, it would appear that all three outcomes are equally likely to win, so you would assign a success probability of 33.3333% to each move. However, in terms of Bayesian probabilities, if you knew from past games that your opponent always started with paper on the first try, you would have a 100% probability of beating him or her if you used scissors as your first move. If your opponent could be expected to put out a rock 50% of the time, then your probability of winning would be 50% if you always put out paper. In practice, people usually make adjustments as they go through a series of decisions, so the Bayesian probabilities will change, but the point is that this technique gives you an advantage due to prior knowledge.

When I was a youth I played the card game Gin Rummy with my mother. Her technique was to always discard high-point face cards that were not needed first so that if she lost the hand she would be caught with fewer points that were not melded. Because I knew of this tendency, I increased my probability of winning by holding face cards during the early stages of the hand in hopes that she would discard a card I wanted. Usually, this knowledge helped, but when she had a good hand and went out early, she would catch me with a lot of points from the face cards!

Whenever you have prior knowledge think in terms of Personal Probabilities instead of Mathematical Probabilities, and it will give you an advantage. For instance in making investments you are more likely to succeed with a stock of an industry or company with which you are very familiar than with one from a company which has a catchy name but about which you know nothing. As another example, I know that in Chicago there is a popular female newspaper columnist named Michael; if I were to make a wager with someone about that person's gender, I would have a definite advantage over someone who thought that the name Michael was used only for males.

There are many strategies for decisions during the course of a game:

- Decisions may be made based on the logic of the game. This type of decision is especially common during a rapid action/reaction game like Ping-Pong or computer video games. There is very little time between moves to think, so reflexes take over in making individual decisions. Prior to playing the game one might consider a new strategy based upon having played the game before, but reflexes and concentration are the chief guides to decision-making during this type of game.

- Decisions may be influenced by knowledge of the way your opponent plays the game. This technique applies whether your opponent is a person or a computer. One example of this is the earlier description of how I played Gin Rummy with my mother. Another is a version of the dice game Yacht that is played against the computer. In this traditional game you use five dice to make poker hands. In the computer version, the computer has been programmed to always try to get a straight sequence before it tries to get multiples of the numbers one through six on the dice. Because straight sequences are difficult to achieve, the computer ends up taking small multiples of the numbers as a consolation prize whenever it fails to make a straight. You can almost always beat the computer by going after the number multiples first and going after the straights later. There are many games of different types where knowledge of the opponent's style of play can give you an advantage in making your decisions. This applies to both individual and team games.

- Decisions can be influenced by how well you and your opponent understand the game. One example of this is Chess, where I could never beat my college roommate because I played as a novice to whom Chess was not a very important contest, while he played with a lot of background in the strategies of the game and with intense concentration.

Team sports are games that require detailed knowledge of every aspect of the contest including rules, strategies and tactics. They also require players with specialized talents and the understanding of how to make people like to work together rather than acting as a group of individuals. In team sports you make decisions about the way to get the most out of the execution of your play assignment, but that assignment may be changed or directed by a coach or manager. Decisions and coordination at both levels are required to win consistently.

- Decisions in games may be based on understanding of what is happening during the playing of the game. Most of us lack sufficient intensity of concentration to be really good at a game or sport. Those who can take in every detail, remember it, and analyze it as the game progresses will tend to make very good decisions and win. One sports example drawing upon this intensity of concentration is the coach of a basketball team. He has the freedom to make frequent changes during the course of a fast-paced game, and he has to be conscious of the level of play of every player in order to make his changes have the desired impact on the course of the game. Another specialist in awareness of what is happening during the course of a game is the gambler who counts cards at a Blackjack table in a casino. Those individuals who have learned this skill are so good at it that they are generally banned from casinos if their card counting is detected. They win because they know what cards are still available at any time, and they don't take unnecessary chances in their betting. Competition Bridge players tell their partners about the strengths and weaknesses of their hands during the bidding process. They also have strategies for responding to any lead by the opposition and have a fairly accurate understanding of who holds what cards at any time. As is the case with high-level Chess players, they continue to study the strategies of championship players throughout their playing careers. All such effort is aimed at getting an edge over their opponents through knowledge of successful approaches and a more complete awareness of what is happening during any particular game.

- Decisions during a game may be influenced by a desire to cheat or to win at any cost. Games and sports have detailed rules which you are expected to follow while you play. Some people want to win at any cost, and they cheat if they can get away with it. In professional sports where a lot of money is involved, such cheating is a great temptation. Accordingly, all of the major professional sports and the Olympics have official staff members whose whole job is to watch for attempts to cheat. Such cheating is usually done in order to guarantee a particular outcome for a game while convincing the public that they are watching a fair contest. Examples of cheating are athletes who take performance-enhancing drugs, and boxers and jockeys who deliberately lose a fight or a race so that gamblers will win by betting on the underdog.

There are other examples that are not outright cheating, but are creative attempts to gain an advantage by doing something that is not specifically against the rules. During early organized baseball, in 1891, Boston Beaneaters star Mike "King" Kelly jumped up off of the team bench to catch a foul ball. As he was jumping up he yelled out, "Kelly now playing for Boston!" Because the baseball rules at that time did not cover this creative situation, he got away with it. However, baseball immediately added a rule requiring all substitutions to be announced or reported to the umpire while the ball was not in play. ("1890's Baseball Timeline", Bowling Green State University, compiled by David R. Haus, Jr.) On August 19, 1951, when Bill Veeck was owner of the St. Louis Browns baseball team, he added Eddie Gaedel, a midget who was 3'7" tall to the team and used him as a pinch hitter in a critical situation. Gaedel was so short that his strike zone in his batting stance crouch was less than two inches vertically, and he walked on four pitches. (www.baseballlibrary.com) Players in most team sports will try to get the best of officiating calls. A running back in football will frequently try to extend his hand holding the football as he is being tackled in the hope that the referee will spot the ball a little farther downfield than he has actually run. Defensive basketball players guarding their basket will readily fall backward when they are hit by an offensive player trying to score because this will frequently draw a charging foul against the offense. Wherever the ruling of a sports official is subjective, players will do anything they can to influence the official's call to favor them. One of their favorite techniques is to emphatically argue against a close ruling on which they are wrong in the belief that the official will later make a close ruling in their favor to offset the earlier ruling and appear fair to both sides. Even Bridge players try to get away with communication signals between partners, but in competitions, officials are very alert for such tricks, which may lead to disqualification or other penalties.

- Decisions in games may be influenced by a desire to have someone else win. We previously discussed the situation of outright cheating by "throwing" a fight or a race in order to let gamblers win money. There is the *slightly* more ethical situation of someone letting the opponent win when no money is involved. This may be a matter of diplomacy, when you feel your boss will treat you better if he wins, or it might be a matter of making a child feel better about himself or herself through your playing ineptly. There is a wide spectrum of such situations; some are more ethical than others. The salesman who loses at golf in order to get a big order from his opponent customer is a lot less ethical than the backyard basketball player who deliberately misses a shot while competing with a child. The salesman is expecting to get a reward for his action, while the basketball player is just trying to make his opponent feel better and more self-confident. However, the important thing to remember about making the decision to lose in any setting is that *such a decision converts the game from a contest to a charade.*

Chapter 11
Multiple Possibility Decisions

There are many instances when you have to make a decision selected from a large number of alternate options. This type of decision may seem difficult or even overwhelming to you when you first face it. In practice there are two approaches to handling multiple alternative subjective decisions. We will discuss the "Divide and Conquer" approach here, and we will discuss the "Subjective Mathematics" approach later when we discuss the allocation of scarce resources.

In the "Divide and Conquer" method of deciding among many decision possibilities, we nibble away at a large challenging problem to make it a smaller one. The first part of this process is to use priority-setting to eliminate those decision possibilities that are either obviously unsuitable or with which you are immediately uncomfortable. This step is the inverse of the way we used priorities earlier. If, for instance, there were ten possible decisions that we could make in a situation, we might find that two were unsuitable because they required a large investment, and one made you uncomfortable because it required you to lie to your best friend. Without having had to assign priorities to all ten possible choices, you have now eliminated three to which you can give the lowest rankings: eight, nine, and ten. There are now seven possible decisions left. The next step is to apply Davidson's Doctrine one choice at a time. If you assume that you have already made any one of the seven remaining choices (at random) you can think through the consequences of that choice and either conclude that it makes you comfortable and is acceptable to you, or that it gives you problems which make it unacceptable. If the first test choice is not acceptable, you now have only six choices left. Repeat the process to see whether your next choice will be acceptable, and if it is not, you will be down to five alternate choices.

Remember that under the section on Corollaries to Davidson's Doctrine, we said that in most situations of multiple possibilities there is more than one acceptable answer. If this is the case in the current situation, you may soon find a reasonable decision after eliminating just a few alternate possibilities. However, for purposes of explaining the examination process, let us assume that there are not multiple acceptable choices in this case.

The next tool we use in our multiple option analysis is a modified version of the "Sherlock Holmes Principle". Arthur Conan Doyle had his consulting detective, Sherlock Holmes, state that in attempting to solve a crime, if you eliminate all but one solution as incorrect, that final solution, however strange, must be the correct one. In trying to choose among a large number of alternate decision possibilities, we are not solving a crime, so we have to modify the "Sherlock Holmes Principle" slightly. If we assume that there are not multiple acceptable choices, we have to say that if we eliminate all but one choice, *the best decision is either the final possible choice or no decision at all.* In effect, we are saying that "no decision" is one possibility in every set of options. If it is the only one which you can assume to have made that makes you comfortable, then "no decision" is the proper choice.

Review the steps in this multiple option analysis until you feel familiar with them. The important principle is that you can analyze one choice at a time rather than having to select among all possible decision options in one step. The process will become almost automatic once you have been through it a few times.

Chapter 12
Reversing Decisions

Decisions are not carved in stone. There are many occasions when you will feel that it is appropriate to reverse a decision that you have previously made. When you do decide that you should reverse a decision, you should not feel guilty about doing so. The analysis that made the reversal an appropriate action is probably just as valid as the analysis that led to the original decision. There are many reasons for reversing a decision. Just a few of them are:

- Changes in comfort with the decision
- Changes in your life situation
- Changes in your priorities
- Reaction to changes made by others in response to your initial decision
- The passage of time
- Environmental changes

There are other reasons that are equally valid, but we will restrict our discussion to these, which will cover most decision reversals.

Davidson's Doctrine is based upon your feeling enough comfort with an assumed subjective decision that you convert it into a real one. This principle of personal comfort with a choice is very important. Consequently, when you become uncomfortable with the results of an earlier decision, it is time to make some kind of change. That change might vary from a slight adjustment in what you are doing, as when NASA makes a mid-course correction of a rocket's path as it heads toward another planet, to a complete reversal of your initial decision.

There will be decisions that yield unexpected results that interfere with your personal comfort by denying you satisfaction. Even in these cases, you can approach comfort by making choices to minimize the discomfort. One example might be your decision to plant a vegetable garden in a corner of your property. Upon breaking up the top layer of soil, you discover that your proposed garden area is full of big rocks and chunks of old concrete. At this point, you may want to modify your original decision and change your project from a vegetable garden to a rock garden with flowers and plants that will grow in barren soil. You won't get your desired vegetables, but you will achieve some sense of accomplishment.

Decisions may require reversal when your life situation changes. Such changes may involve marriage or divorce, a health problem, loss of a job, bankruptcy, natural disaster, or a legal problem. We build our plans upon the strengths of our situation at the time of our initial decision, and we assume that they will remain stable. Sometimes they do, but when major changes to our status occur, we must be ready to consider alternate directions for our future growth.

You usually encounter changes in your life situation due to external forces. However, you may also feel that it is necessary to reverse an earlier decision due to your own actions in changing your priorities and goals. Things that were important to you before may lose their value relative to other objectives.

I once read a story about problems in introducing a branch of a large western corporation into a country with a culture based on the following of traditional practices. The corporation expected that all of their local employees would act like the staff members at their industrialized headquarters location and that they would work to improve their standard of living by becoming more and more efficient at their assignments over many years. Instead, management was surprised and disappointed to find that many of their workers quit after a relatively short period of time. When management interviewed the departing workers, they found the common reason for leaving to be that the workers had acquired what they considered a sufficiently large amount of money. Now they wanted to return to their villages. Their attitude was that the money, which was their initial goal, had grown to the point where it could now be a tool to allow them to spend more time with their families in somewhat better living conditions. The workers expected that they would stay home until the money ran out and that they would then return to the corporation to work and earn some more money and repeat the process. Initially, money had been the top priority, but once money was available, time with their families became the top priority. This attitude of the employees was difficult for the corporation's management to understand, and it caused a reversal of the decision to establish the new branch plant in that country. This situation is one example of the need to understand the culture of the people with whom you are working. We will discuss this further in a later chapter.

Another case where a change in priorities might require a decision reversal might occur when someone is graduated from college and makes plans for starting a first career job in the expectation that she will make a total break with her past background. When she learns that her father has become seriously ill, she realizes that she will have to return home to run the family business. Career formerly was the highest priority, but now family and the family business have become higher priorities requiring a reversal of her career decision.

You may find it desirable to reverse your original decision in reaction to what others did in response to your decision. This brings to mind Newton's law of physics that says that for every action there is an equal and opposite reaction. One example of this situation would involve your move in Chess that is countered by your opponent's move that puts you into a state of "check". You would have to respond to the opponent's move by either reversing your original move or making another move to get out of "check". A second example would   be your expressed interest in purchasing a car or a piece of jewelry, that might have to be reversed after you are told how much more expensive it is than you had expected.

The passage of time might cause you to reverse a decision as in the case when you make an offer for the purchase of a new house on the basis of a predicted date of completion, and you later find that its scheduled completion has been delayed by a year. A second example might involve your planned purchase of a large pickup truck or SUV which you decide to reverse because prior to actually getting to the time of purchasing it you realize that it would be a very expensive choice due to rapidly rising gasoline prices.

Environmental changes might cause you to reverse a decision if you had been planning a trip to a place that has just suffered a natural disaster. You also might reverse your decision to plant a garden if the weather turns unseasonably cold or wet.

Chapter 13
Teamwork and Decisions

In many situations decisions are made by a team because of rules, the size or nature of the job to be performed, or because it is obviously more efficient to proceed on a team basis and tackle multiple aspects of the project simultaneously. Examples are sports teams, technical research and development groups, military organizations, and disaster relief organizations (whether formal or informal).

Sports teams are organizations where rules require teamwork in making decisions and acting upon them. Not only is each organization set up as a team, but also each competing team in the sport is set up under identical rules. In other situations you may be acting as a team while your competition is not, but in team sports the same rules and organizations apply to every competing group. This rigid framework allows the leadership of each team to know essentially how the competition will behave. This is true to such an extent that sports teams carefully study films and tapes of their opponents playing in past games in order to predict what they will do in a future contest. Two teams in competition are usually so evenly matched that the winner is usually determined by the side that has slightly more talent; makes the better decisions; introduces the most innovation; and best shares communication of their game plan among the team members. In most sports the team having better decisions, innovation, and communication can overcome a slight deficit in talent to win more frequently than not. This is why management in almost any team sport will try to acquire the services of field managers and coaches with the best histories of having won with other teams. These are the people who can turn a group of talented individuals into a smoothly functioning team and make creative decisions that will increase team effectiveness beyond the sum of the talents of the individual players.

Team effectiveness is also the goal in efforts that are organized to achieve an objective through the use of personnel with specific assigned roles. Such an organization may be a sports team, but it may also be a business, technical, or medical group. Earlier in discussing decisions during negotiations, I described a temporary group with specialized roles that had been brought together by a corporation for the purpose of conducting a specific negotiation process. They had not worked together as a team prior to the negotiation, and they would not do so again afterward. Such specialized teams may be formed on a temporary, periodic, or permanent basis. A medical surgical team with assigned roles would be an example of a group that is periodically brought together whenever a particular surgical procedure is to be performed. A more permanent group requiring specialized teamwork would be a technical research and development organization. This type of group investigates basic or applied science and engineering in order to develop new knowledge, techniques, and devices. Their goal is to increase the level of scientific knowledge and/or develop new products and processes that enhance corporate profitability. Even if such an organization comes up with new scientific knowledge in a purely academic context, great efforts will subsequently be made to find economic applications for the group's results. A technical R&D organization requires many specialized people because it is unlikely that any single individual will know enough about a complex problem being investigated to make wise decisions. Instead, a task force is organized wherein each individual makes decisions and recommendations about his own area of expertise, and final decisions involving several technical areas are coordinated on a consensus basis by the project manager. The project manager also serves as the spokesperson for the R&D group to the management of the sponsoring university or corporation and works to acquire adequate budgeting for the group.

Military organizations consist of people who function within a hierarchy performing specialized functions. In such groups the directions, assignments, and strategies come from someone higher in the organization than the team members who are assigned to perform most of the work. This type of organization works effectively as a team to make decisions when there is clear and enlightened direction from the top of the hierarchy, but it may be difficult for communication to flow upward rather than downward through the organization structure. Military organizations are among the best for organizing large numbers of people into a functioning team, but there may be too many links in the chain of command between the individual who makes a strategic or tactical decision and the individuals who have to execute that decision.

By contrast with the military model, teams tend to work well together without much structure during relief efforts in the aftermath of a disaster. On an overall coordination level organization and planning are extremely important. This is especially true for massive disasters like the Asian tsunami on December 26, 2004 or Hurricane Katrina in August of 2005. However, on a local level response to a disaster tends to be spontaneous, and people who may have lived alongside each other without communicating suddenly become members of a team. As one example, I was visiting someone near the Massachusetts seacoast during a hurricane some years ago, and when we went outside as the storm eased, we discovered that two cars were floating offshore in the Atlantic Ocean. Very quickly and without organizational direction, people converged at the scene, many of them bringing ropes and cables from their cars and homes. Within just a few minutes we had attached ropes to the floating cars, and together with a working group of close to fifty people we were pulling them out of the ocean. This large group of people had become a team spontaneously. They worked together very efficiently, but after the two floating cars had been retrieved the group dispersed and returned to their various homes. Fortunately there had not been any people inside those cars. This incident was an isolated one, but similar spontaneous groups arise in cases like sandbagging against rising floodwaters and searching for missing persons. In many disaster situations diverse groups of people converge to work together on a strictly voluntary and mutual assistance basis without any decision-making hierarchy. Many times in such a context someone has said that it takes a disaster to bring us all together.

Chapter 14
Who's in Charge?

As we have seen from the previous discussion of types of organizations involving the need for teamwork, the true focus of the leadership of the organization can vary greatly. The person who is the effective leader of a group may not even have a title, as was the case for the leader of the informal disaster relief team. For our purposes we will define the effective leader of an organization as the person who makes most of the day-to-day decisions or influences their being made by someone else. In some organizations the formal leader is also the hands-on leader who instigates most of the actions. In others, the formal leader delegates his or her authority to subordinates with specific decision-making authority. However, in many other cases leaders high in the organization make decisions that are only general guidelines, and it is up to those lower in the organization to dot the "I's" and cross the "T's" in order to create the detailed plans that make operations succeed. These people are the effective leaders of the organization, and they may be project leaders, department heads, union stewards, secretaries, or untitled individuals with initiative and insight. In relatively young groups, the effective leadership may change from time to time. In older groups, everyone will usually know exactly whom to contact when decisive action is required. New employees will generally be inclined to work through the person with the grandest title, while veteran employees will go directly to the effective leader for quicker results. Such an effective leader will quickly become what sociologists call a "sociometric star", a term coined by Jacob Moreno. He suggested that we create a diagram or "sociogram" of the organization in which we represent individuals by points and their relationships with each other by lines. The effective leaders become evident if you look for the individuals in the group who have multiple relationship lines radiating from them to other people. These effective leaders are at the center of a pattern that resembles an asterisk because many different people interact with them. Hence the term *star*. In contrast, some of the people with the top titles may interact with only one or two other people. When a study of organizational interactions reveals more than one sociometric star, they may not all be leaders, or they may serve as leaders for different purposes. All sociometric stars are not necessarily effective leaders, but each effective leader will generally be a star.

Sometimes the effective leader is someone who has the confidence of the organization leader, such as an administrative assistant or secretary. In other cases he or she may be the person with the greatest understanding of the business plan or the project which is being undertaken. Gatekeepers who control financial or purchasing approvals or technical equipment specifications may also tend to emerge as stars. Whatever his or her title is, the effective leader shows a great deal of initiative and knowledge of how to make systems and people work together efficiently. If you are not the star in your organization, your easiest path to seeing your decisions yield substantial results is to identify and develop a friendship or good working relationship with the star person who is the effective leader for the project in which you are involved.

Chapter 15
Small and Large Decisions

Decisions come in all sizes, and the time available to make decisions varies also. You face the need to make many small decisions every day, but large decisions are required less frequently. If you were to take time and make a conscious effort for every decision of the day, you would get very little done. The best device for handling the majority of these daily choices (When should I get up? What should I have for breakfast? What should I wear?) is a routine with which you are comfortable. Such a routine can be developed over a period of time with changes made as needed to include or remove tasks and introduce efficiencies. Routines are especially useful early in the day in order to get a quick start before your thinking processes are fully focused. Through the use of routines to handle the smaller choices of the day, you will have more time available to handle the larger decisions. Some people react to routines as being dull, but they are actually very effective tools for minimizing the number of decisions that you have to consciously make. They also allow you to keep your mind relatively free to think of important things beyond the details of the task you are performing.

As an example, when you first learn to drive you devote a great deal of concentration to the mechanical steps of operating an automobile: shifting, steering, peddle pressures, instrument panel control positions, etc. Once you have become an accomplished driver, those mechanical operation decisions are handled subconsciously, allowing you to devote your conscious attention to more important matters like safety and navigating to your destination. Routines allow you to handle the many minimal decisions of each day on a subconscious level. Rules also help eliminate individual decisions on small matters. For example, traffic lights eliminate large numbers of repetitious decisions as to which car should proceed first at an intersection.

The business version of a routine is a procedure. Most businesses of all sizes use procedures in order to have a uniform approach and technique for handling a standard problem. There will be a comprehensive manual of procedures for different tasks and sets of authorized standards for production tasks. Procedures and standards are used to always approach the same problem in the same way, even if different people are assigned to it at different times. Business procedures codify what should be done in handling standard jobs, and they also serve the important legal function of documenting that the company has thought through all implications of its activities. However, as soon as a task becomes non-standard or a change is made to a product, the company has to be ready to make new detailed decisions about how procedures should be varied to accommodate the changes. Even when there are not changes in what has to be done, a well-managed company schedules periodic discussions on how to vary procedures in order to do the existing tasks more efficiently.

One of the problems with large or relatively large decisions is that it is human nature to think that the larger the decision, the more difficult it will be. This is not necessarily the case. We should always look to see whether a large problem requiring a decision could be subdivided into several somewhat smaller problems with their corresponding decisions. Usually, every large effort can be divided into steps, and by working on those steps individually you can reduce the difficulty of the whole effort and the resources required for it. An additional way to reduce the difficulty of a large project is to spread it out over time. Two examples of the "subdivide and spread over time" approaches to handling a major project follow, one personal and one business in nature.

Example: The Challenge of Attending College

The prospect of sending a son or daughter (or yourself) to college and supporting him or her throughout the college years is a scary one. Most reference materials discuss the costs of college in terms of the totals required for one year or four years. In practice, you can divide this problem into much smaller pieces:

- Realize that you don't have to pay for everything at once. A College will bill by the quarter, trimester, or semester depending on the way its school year is divided. It may even have more than one bill deadline during the quarter, trimester, or semester in order to reduce the size of the payment that is due. You have to be ready to make the next payment when it is due, but you then have time to accumulate funds for the following payment before that next due date arrives.

- The admissions process for college is difficult, because colleges want to have the best student body possible and because there are many more applicants than there are openings available for them. Once a student has been accepted to a college, the administration will do everything in its power to make that student succeed. This is called "The Gatekeeper Phenomenon". Admissions people carefully select incoming students, but having selected them, the administration will encourage and support them because they want to show that they had made good choices in admitting them and because each class once selected contributes less revenue to the college if its members drop out. The loss of class members is also a signal that the teaching process is not working well. Because the administration serves as a gatekeeper, it will be more willing to give a low cost loan or a scholarship to a student who is already a member of the class than to someone who is only an applicant. Once your student has been admitted, and you have paid one or two bills, apply for additional student aid. You have nothing to lose by applying, and you may be pleasantly surprised by the results. Colleges once strictly pegged financial aid to the need of the applicant. In recent years many of them have restructured their programs to be blind to the level of need in order to make aid equally available to all students.

- Once your student begins classes, encourage him or her to make an intense effort to do well on grades during the first quarter or semester. If the student does well and has good grades to show when applying for additional financial aid, the school is very likely to grant it. Your student has become a success story for them. This process has also brought your successful student to the attention of the administration in a way that will be likely to have valuable results if the student applies for future opportunities of any sort. I used this technique in graduate school where I had entered with a very limited amount of savings. The first quarter I overloaded on courses and received good grades in all of them. After that, I received full-tuition scholarships for the balance of my stay so that I only had to cover my living expenses and supplies.

- Once your student has become acclimated to workloads and college life, consider having him or her take on a part-time job. Every college has many of these available, some of which are quite educational such as working for a professor on a research project. Private business jobs usually yield better pay than student jobs on a research project, but the latter look good on a resume when your student applies for a full-time position after graduation. Research projects with a professor pay more in prestige than in money.

- If the foregoing steps are not sufficient, along with the budget you have available, to cover the costs of college, there are at least two other resources available. You can apply for a government-insured or personal loan at a commercial bank or you can investigate whether the college has a Cooperative Education Plan available. A "co-op" student works for private business or industry for several months during which period he or she earns pay at reasonable rates while also receiving formal recognition for the experience gained. The formal recognition could take the form of a grade, awarding of credit hours, satisfaction of a degree requirement, or a notation on the student's transcript. Following this work period the student returns to campus for academic courses having the funds from the work period for financial support. This alternation of business experience and academic periods is repeated until the student has enough credits for graduation. The co-op plan usually extends the time required before graduation, but it is a self-funding process for the student, and it lets the graduating student show a body of work experience on his or her resume. Usually, the work assignments are varied and sequenced to coordinate with the curriculum that leads to the degree. The work experience gained while going to college in a co-op program could make it easier for the student to find a full-time position than would be the case for a purely academic student without work experience.

- One final approach to reducing the burden of college is to have the student apply for one of the financial incentives offered by the military services. This approach will appeal to relatively few students, and it carries a military service obligation with it. However, this is an available source of funding to carry the student through graduation if other sources are insufficient.

The point of the foregoing college education discussion is to show that seemingly huge problems can be subdivided or spread out over time so that at any point you are only faced with a relatively small problem and the correspondingly simpler decision as to how to solve it.

Example: Start-up of a Small Business

A second situation involving the tackling of a large problem on a step-by-step basis is the start-up of a small business. When I first looked into the possibility of starting my own business and leaving the security of a large corporation, I was told that I needed a minimum of $500,000.00 to be reasonably sure of being able to stay in business long enough to be successful. I neither had this amount of money nor did I have any prospect of getting someone to give it to me. Instead, when I decided to make the attempt, I cashed in my profit sharing vested interest at the company that I was leaving. This gave me a bank balance of $6,000.00. I then started the business working out of my home so that I would have no rent, and I took no salary for the first year. During the first seven months of operations we took in a grand total of $2,800.00 in gross receipts. The next year we had billings of about ten times that amount, and after that it became somewhat easier. Throughout the life of the company we purchased used equipment whenever possible, ordered only quantities of goods sufficient for immediate projects, and diligently returned excess purchases for credit. Your goal in a start-up business is to survive and to be self-sustaining based on revenues from sales. When you start with a very small amount of capital you do your best to minimize overhead and capital expenses in order to reduce the sales level at which you become sustainable. During the course of seminars I attended prior to starting the business, I learned that a small business that survives for ten years can probably keep going for as long as it desires to do so. I also learned that just a few percent of small businesses do survive for ten years. This does not mean that your business will be a big success after ten years. You may not grow very much, or you may exceed your expectations greatly. In one form or another the business will tend to survive well beyond ten years if you have made enough good decisions, and you have developed a good family of products and services and a large enough customer base.

Sometimes small decisions take longer to make than large ones. In business, the budget discussions for office supplies can be longer than the debates over buying a major piece of production equipment. This occurs because everyone claims to be an expert on office supplies, while only a few specialists can judge the sophisticated production device. The latter item may also have been supported by a technical or planning study document.

On a personal level, finding the perfect small gift for someone can take a lot of discussion and shopping, both at stores and on the Internet. In contrast to this, I bought my latest car while I was in for an oil change for the old one because I thought that it was time for a change and because I wanted the safety upgrades featured in the new version. This was apparently a snap decision, but I had been considering the vehicle change subconsciously for quite a while, and I was ready to convert my assumed decision into a real one when the opportunity arose.

The point of these examples is that in some instances there is no correspondence between the magnitude or material value of a decision and the time required in preparation for that choice. This is especially true in a crisis situation where life-and-death decisions must be made very quickly.

Chapter 16
Decisions and Planning

Planning a future project or any other long-term activity sounds as though it should be a very difficult and daunting task. This is especially true because planning concerns future events, and they rarely turn out the way we expect. *Actually, planning is nothing more than a repetitive application of the assumed decision process that we have been using and advocating.*

Whenever you make a plan, you start with a first assumed decision in the same way that the philosophical thousand-mile journey starts with a single step. If, for instance, you are planning to retire fifteen years from now, you might make the first assumed decision that you should put $100.00 per month into a special savings account. This account would earn interest and would also give you working capital that could be withdrawn in favor of other investments or a down payment on a retirement home. In reviewing this first assumed decision, you would quickly discover by doing the math that at the end of fifteen years you would have deposited only $18,000.00 into the account and that even with interest at anything close to current rates your deposits would not have doubled by retirement time. You might then make the assumed decision that you would start by depositing $100.00 per month, but that each year you would increase the monthly deposit by $25.00. This approach would give you deposits of $49,500.00 at the end of fifteen years plus the accumulated interest, which brings the total to a much more significant figure.

You could turn this revised deposit plan into an actual decision and then make a new assumed decision that you would take a certain percentage of the accumulated deposits out each year. You might assume that you would invest the withdrawn savings into a mutual fund so that you would have both insured savings and market-based securities working toward your retirement. You might also make the assumed decision that you would increase your contribution amount in each year that your salary rose by more than inflation and decrease it in years when your salary did not keep up with inflation.

This example is included to show that our assumed decision process works well with long-term planning, because we have to make assumptions in dealing with the future. We know that some of those assumptions will be wrong, but we have learned how to analyze the results of an assumed decision and to make periodic modifications as required.

We can be fairly certain about what is happening now, so the first step in our planning process will tend to be a good one with relatively expectable results. As we look further into the future our accuracy will continually decrease. In the case of the retirement planning example we should expect that bank interest rates would turn out to be higher or lower than assumed. The mutual fund money invested in the stock market would likely have growth that is higher or lower than we expected. Because of our lack of knowledge about the future, we should bracket our expected plan results with an error allowance that shows a range from worst case to best case for each time period. Our expected result should lie in between these extremes, and the error bracketing should increase in magnitude as we look further into the future because we have less and less certainty as we look further away. Most companies do not even attempt to make business plans much further out than three to five years because of increasing uncertainty. Retirement plans necessarily have to be long-term, but you should not count on your early expectations, and you should review your status and plans periodically.

The old saying, "The best-laid plans of mice and men oft go astray" is true in more ways than one. Sometimes it means that your plans have to be revised many times in order to reach your original goal, but sometimes the deviations from original expectations lead you to a destination that is much more interesting and desirable. Life may be more rewarding if you are open to this possibility.

Chapter 17
Morality and Conscience in Decision-Making

Davidson's Doctrine advocates using your personal comfort with the perceived and expected results and consequences of an assumed decision as the criterion for actually making that decision after thinking it through. This principle assumes that the decisions you reach through the assumed decision process will be based upon ethics and morality. Hopefully that will be the case, but even people who are amoral or immoral may find themselves deterred from bad decisions through the process if their analysis of the expected results of their assumed decision suggests consequences that they are not willing to risk. People have different degrees of ethics and may have different variations of a moral code and conscience depending on their backgrounds and their current position in the social order. At least the assumed decision process gives everyone a chance to think about the possible implications of a decision before committing to it.

Whatever a person's level of morality, it will have some effect on the decision-making process. Morality is a function of both inherited and personally developed values. People have a combination of the values that their family and religion have taught them and the values that they have gained from their personal and observed experiences.

When you try to anticipate the effects of your decisions on others, your analysis will lead to more accurate opinions if you have knowledge of the moral outlook of those whom your decisions will affect. Their values may not be the same as yours, but they are likely to be just as deeply held. It is easier to predict the reaction to your decision of someone with a different moral code than yours than it is to anticipate the reaction of someone with no moral code at all. At one time societies were more traditional and more closely governed by inherited moral values. As people have become more individualistic and separated from their family and societal traditions, there has been an accompanying growth of litigation to resolve disputes that were once simply governed by morality and traditional values. Western societies have become so litigious that very few government, corporate, and even personal decisions of significant magnitude can now be made without consulting an attorney. Such considerations of legal aspects are a matter of self-protection because of the tendencies of individuals and groups to pursue a lawsuit whenever there is an unexpected consequence of an agreement or a decision.

Once again, I suggest that you return to the question of comfort with a decision. Sometimes during the course of business I have found myself having a customer whose ethics made me uncomfortable, either because of the nature of the customer's business or because of the way that he or she interacted with me or with my company. In every case where this occurred and involved repeated transactions, I told the customer that we did not want to work with them any more. The customer is not always right. There are times when you have to fire a customer with whom you are uncomfortable so that you can give better service to your other customers. Similarly, if you don't feel comfortable with the business practices of a vendor, start searching for an alternate vendor who can do the job and give you a dependable relationship also.

Chapter 18
Personal and Societal Decisions

Occasionally, there are differences between the goals of society and your personal or family goals. This is not always the case; usually what is good for you is good for your society and vice versa.

Conflicts may arise when society wants to ration scarce resources, and you want as large a share of those resources as you can get. This is especially significant as people and societies discuss measures that can and should be taken to offset the Global Warming climate changes that have become evident around the world. Many people and agencies are developing lists of steps that *could* be taken to minimize climate change. The big question is whether enough individuals *would* follow the procedures that societies recommend. Many would undoubtedly try to maximize their personal wellbeing now and would ignore future consequences of their actions. Another way to look at the Global Warming situation is that some governments have refused to believe it is real. As more and more individuals talk about it and take personal steps to reduce the effects of climate change, all governments will have to accept the truth of Global Warming or they will lose the support of their voters.

Other conflicts may involve relationships with other countries, such as when the government is moving toward a war, and you want peace if at all possible because you have children who would probably have to fight in that war. You might also differ with the government's outlook on health services, taxes, and degree of legal regulation of your life style. The important thing to realize is that both you and the society have needs that are important to satisfy, and that you may both be correct from your points of view, but your goals may be incompatible.

When the needs of the society and the individual are in conflict, some form of compromise or accommodation is required if the society is to remain stable and respected by its people and by other peer and competing societies. When a conflict arises with a relatively small number of individuals, the easiest solution is for the society to allow those few to make decisions that do not match those of the society. That is why our legislatures frequently enact laws that are not enforced in the short term. However, when the conflict spreads to a very large number of individuals, the society must take some kind of action to reach a compromise. One example of this situation would be that if gasoline prices were rising rapidly, and a relatively small number of people wanted to drive low-efficiency gas-guzzling cars and trucks, there would not be much problem for the government to allow them to do so. However, if the majority of individuals made the same decision, it would drive the price of gasoline upward even more rapidly, and the government would either have to enact and enforce higher fuel efficiency standards, or it would have to ration the gas-guzzling vehicles or place limits on their use. Alternatively, the government could ration gasoline in order to minimize the use of the gas-guzzling vehicles and convince some owners to replace them with more fuel-efficient models.

There are other possible illustrations, but the principle is that there are times when you will want to make a decision that is in conflict with a government or societal decision or goal. There are some goals that can only be achieved by the society as a whole such as going to the moon or curing a major disease, but in some cases society will have some goals that are unnecessarily in conflict with those of the individual. For instance, the government's goal of staying out of the healthcare marketplace may be unnecessarily in conflict with the individual's goal of being able to purchase reasonably priced health insurance and prescriptions.

When personal vs. societal conflicts exist, it is very important that they be resolved creatively. The individual must be at least somewhat satisfied and the society must be unified enough to turn its attention to dealings with the rest of the world rather than devoting all its efforts to handling internal dissension. If enough individuals differ with the government on an issue and make their disagreement widely known, the government may be forced to modify it's outlook either through influence of the conflict upon legislators or through the results of subsequent elections. There is nothing that influences a legislator more than the likelihood that he or she will not be reelected.

Chapter 19
Religion and Culture in Decisions

One factor that influences the way you make decisions is <u>who you are</u>. This sounds as though it should require only a simple statement of identity, but there are many ingredients to describing yourself:

- Nationality: I have never been able to figure out why people who have been born in the United States frequently say that they are the nationality (or nationalities) of their ancestors rather than that they are Americans.
- Race: Hopefully this label has diminishing importance with time.
- Religion: What you believe (or a belief you reject) affects your thinking during decision-making.
- Upbringing: Were you raised by one parent or by two? Were your parents strict,

tolerant, or too preoccupied to notice your behavior?

- Occupation: This means not just your current occupation, but every job you have ever had and the career for which you were trained, even if you never practiced it.
- Gender: Men and women do think differently about many things.
- Age: Are you hoping to learn about history, or have you already lived it?
- Education: (And equally important, Intelligence, which is not the same thing.)
- Experience: Are you facing a type of decision for the first time, or have you made many such decisions before?
- Marital Status: Marital responsibilities change your outlook.
- Parental Status: Parental responsibilities change your outlook.
- Sociability: Are you an introvert or an extrovert?
- Trauma: Have you ever had traumatic experiences? Are you in the midst of one now?
- Physical Condition: Are you healthy or trying to overcome a health problem?
- And many other miscellaneous factors...

Now, having seen this list, are you able to say who you are? The answer is probably that even though you know more about yourself than anyone else does, you cannot give a definitive answer to this question. If you could give an answer, it would be likely to be different from the answer that you would give next week or that you would have given last week. We do not know ourselves completely, and our feelings about ourselves change with time. This is one reason why our outlooks and decisions tend to be inconsistent over time and why we change our minds. Our feelings about ourselves vary, and that makes our priorities vary as well.

Despite the fact that we find it difficult to define ourselves, we seem to be able to define and label other people quite readily. We don't allow for the possibility that they are individuals with complex personalities in the same way that we are. This is one of the root causes of prejudice as well as interpersonal and international conflicts. We put anyone who is perceived to be different out of the "we" category and into the "they" category. Religion and culture are two of the main inputs for defining who belongs to the "we" group and who belongs to the "they" group. We may have different viewpoints and make different decisions depending on whether they involve our relationships with "we" people or with "they" people. To the extent that we can relate to others as complex individuals, we can remove them from the "they" category and diminish the importance of the "they" label.

Beyond affecting our views toward people who are perceived to be different, religion and culture help to determine our outlook with regard to values, ethics, and goals. Our specific beliefs and backgrounds help to determine whether we will feel comfortable with the expected consequences of a particular assumed decision. This context may make us much more or much less likely to decide to go through with a decision we are contemplating. Being more comfortable with people of your own beliefs and backgrounds is one reason why such similar people tend to live near each other and to have similar occupations. The grouping of similar people in this way may make it easier to make compatible decisions with neighbors and business associates, but it extends the feeling of "we" vs. "they" from individuals to larger social aggregations. The best ways to ease decision-making among people with dissimilar backgrounds are to:

- Learn as much as possible about the customs of other groups.
- Treat people from those groups as individuals rather than as members of a uniform entity.
- Concentrate on similarities rather than differences between you.
- Cultivate appreciation and respect for their values and traditions.
- Say or do something their way rather than yours to build bridges between you.

Some societies are relatively homogeneous because they consist almost entirely of people from one ethnic group with the same religion and culture. Members of such a society have high comfort levels in making decisions that affect each other. Some societies are segmented, having many different relatively large groups, each of which contains people with similar backgrounds and beliefs. Members of this type of society may find decisions easy to make within their own segmental group, but more difficult when the decision involves people from another such group. Other societies are "atomized", having individual people of multiple backgrounds and beliefs living and working alongside each other without the stabilizing benefits of families and traditions. In such societies there may be less of a feeling of "we" and "they", allowing a higher comfort level with decisions that involve other people. However, atomized societies require continuous attention to equal treatment for all people, or they will not give their individual members a sense of loyalty and belonging. Unequal treatment of individuals who do not feel part of the group could lead to disaffection, instability, and rebellion. Regardless of the size of a social group, whether it is a family, a business, a college, or a country, it is easier to make decisions in an atmosphere of stability than in one of confrontation and chaos. Instability makes too many considerations change at the same time, requiring you to consider more alternative possibilities during the process of making a decision.

Chapter 20
The Time Dimension of Decisions

A decision will be more or less correct or valuable depending on when it is made. In some cases a decision made at the wrong time will have no value at all. The simplest example of this may be a baseball batter who hesitates before making his decision and swings at a pitched ball that has already passed him. Another example is the proverbial action of locking the barn door after the horse has already been stolen. In this case you might feel some satisfaction in keeping someone from breaking into the barn in the future, but if you only had one horse, locking the barn door after its theft accomplishes nothing.

Business decisions frequently vary in value depending on timing. It is very difficult to buy stocks at the specific time when they are moving upward from their lowest value, or to sell them at the moment when they are moving downward from their peak price. Nobody is quite sure whether a slight change in price is the beginning of a major change or just a temporary variation. Successful investors may be good at recognizing the conditions for a significant change in price of a stock, but they either have anticipate the change with an advance purchase or sale, or they have to react very rapidly once the fact of a price change becomes obvious.

A car salesperson will frequently ask, "What price do I have to give you for you to buy this car today?" If you leave without making a purchase, it is likely that you won't buy the car at all, so a decision today is much more valuable to him or her than one at some time in the future. It is even more valuable than your possible decision to come back and make a purchase within the next few days, because at that time you might work with a different salesperson who would get the commission instead of the original individual. In such a price negotiation, the longer you give the seller the impression that you are not sufficiently interested to buy the car, the lower the final purchase price is likely to be. This means that in this situation delaying your decision has value. There is a variation in the value of your decision with time.

In a labor negotiation, a final agreement will almost always happen at the last minute, just before a strike walkout is about to happen. Both sides know that going beyond that point will cost them a lot of money and possibly prestige. They also know that they are not likely to get the best offer from the other side until the deadline has been reached.

Another aspect of the time dimension of decisions is that some decisions will have short-term value; others will have long-term value; and some will have both short and long-term value. For example, when a father decides to take his young child fishing, that decision leads to the short-term value of some quality time together. If, in the process the child learns how to fish, the decision to go fishing has produced long-term value as well. Additional short-term value will result if they catch some fish!

History, whether personal or societal, has an effect on our decisions. If you have been in a traffic accident recently, you drive differently than you did before. You tend to drive as though a potential accident is around every corner. Eventually, this sort of tentativeness and sense of foreboding goes away, but it takes a substantial amount of time and repetition.

The timing of decisions is very important when the decision involves technology. If you are looking to buy a computer, experts advise you not to purchase a unit that has the very latest technology, because the newest computers and software may have "bugs" in them that have not yet been identified and resolved. The experts suggest instead that you purchase a product based on last year's technology because enough time will have passed for the problems to be cured while the level of technology will still be relatively high. On the other hand, computer technology changes so rapidly that your purchase decision has to include consideration of whether you are purchasing a product that is already obsolete. Sometimes it is a matter of balancing technology against cost. The price of last year's technology will generally be less than that for the latest model. The same thing applies in purchasing a car. You can save substantially by making your purchase decision at the end of the model year rather than at the beginning. Cars purchased at the beginning or the end of the model year will have the same model year designation. The early purchaser will have had the pleasure of driving a current year car for a longer time, but the person who buys at the end of the year will have paid less, and his/her car will be substantially newer, with less wear and tear on it.

Chapter 21
Resource Allocation Decisions

Whether you are creating a household budget or considering seventy possible projects for a corporation, you are facing a problem of allocating your resources for the best total results.

In almost all cases you will have limited resources to use in trying to accomplish your desired objectives. The problem is simple if you are trying to do only one task; you can potentially use all available resources for it. When you are faced with a large number of pending tasks or obligations, it is necessary to do some analysis in order to decide what resources to use for each possible commitment. Because resources are limited, there may be some desired commitments that you will have to postpone or delete from your list.

The first question in considering resource allocation is: "What resources do I have?" Many things can be resources, but some types will not be needed for every project or obligation. Typical resources that you might be allocating are:

- Cash that you have on hand or in the bank
- Credit availability
- Labor that you can perform
- Labor that would have to be supplied by others
- Time (a very limited resource which must be divided up wisely)
- Materials that may be required
- Computer services
- Manufacturing production equipment time
- Media production equipment time
- Transportation services and equipment

Given that you have resources that can be allocated to different tasks, you should ask:

- Which tasks have the most importance?
- What resources are required for each task?
- How many tasks can I accomplish with the set of resources that I have?
- What is the cost of each task?
- What is the value of each task?

These questions sound difficult and complicated, but we will simplify the process of obtaining answers to them. Subjective Mathematics is the tool we will use to simplify the process. We discussed earlier the setting of priorities to help you decide the relative importance of various tasks. Subjective Mathematics can be used to quantify the setting of priorities and to give you a more tangible feeling for the relative values of different tasks when you are considering many different possibilities. Usually, we will use Subjective Mathematics to assign relative values to the various tasks while also considering their relative costs. This process will give us a relatively clear idea of what we would like to do, but we have to follow it up by determining the resources that would be required for each desired task. The process might indicate that there are twelve tasks that we definitely want to accomplish, but if we have only enough resources for ten of them, the two lowest priority tasks will have to be deferred until we have more resources available.

The Subjective Mathematics tool may be applied using a computer spreadsheet program for complicated project comparisons or a simple table on paper for relatively simple projects. The approach is to list the various alternate tasks that you are considering in a vertical column of a table and to list various categories of value and cost at the tops of columns to the right of the task column. We can fill in relative levels of value and cost in the rows of boxes to the right of each task. We can use a rating scale of one to ten to show how we feel about each aspect of each project. Value items are given a positive rating, while cost items are given a negative rating.

The subjective part of this system is that you decide the relative ratings depending on your current feelings and priorities. If anyone else were to do the ratings, he or she would probably rate the tasks differently, as might you if you were rating them at a different point in time. You are going to have to decide on allocation of your resources in such a way that use of your personal ratings will maximize your personal comfort with the results. If your viewpoint changes or external events require it, you can repeat the rating process at any time, yielding possibly different results. At the end of the rating process you add across the numbers in each row algebraically, plus for a value item rating and minus for a cost item rating to get your final overall ratings of each task or project.

Here is an example table based on a household budgeting allocation problem. It has a limited number of boxes, so it may not be representative of a real situation. The first three columns with numbers are values and are positive. The next three columns with numbers are costs and are negative.

BUDGET	NEED	DESIRE	USEFUL	(DIRECT COST)	(ADD-ON COSTS)	(LOAN OR FINANCE)	NET RATING
NEW CAR	3	8	8	-10	-8	-10	-9 (#7)
COMPUTER	4	8	9	-7	-5	-5	+4 (#6)
CLOTHING	10	6	10	-6	-3	-4	+13 (#4)
GIFTS	8	8	5	-5	-0	-2	+14 (#3)
FOOD	10	8	10	-7	-0	-0	+21 (#1)
FURNACE	10	7	10	-8	-0	-5	+14 (#3)
INSURANCE	10	7	8	-6	-0	-3	+16 (#2)
TAXES	10	6	7	-6	-0	-3	+14 (#3)
TOOLS	5	7	9	-6	-2	-3	+10 (#5)

In the example shown in the table, we had three positive value categories and three negative cost categories. The categories you use will depend on the type of tasks or projects you are comparing. They will be much more detailed for a business project comparison than for a personal one. The Subjective Mathematics approach to resource allocation decisions gets its strength from the fact that it uses your personal viewpoint in rating each item and from its use of multiple ratings of details to build up to the final answer. In the sample chart above, we had a three-way tie for third place, but each of the third place items was rated differently. The sequence of the final ratings for the household budget came out:

1. Food
2. Insurance
3. Gifts / Furnace / Taxes
4. Clothing
5. Tools
6. Computer
7. New Car

This is a reasonable result for many households and situations. However, the ratings might have been greatly different if you had been rating the same set of options with the knowledge that your car had just been in a bad accident and that your furnace was in good working condition. This type of rating system is only as good as the knowledge that you bring to it. You have to be honest with yourself when using this tool, because you can force the ratings to prefer a certain result if you have a strong bias toward or away from something. When such a bias becomes obvious, it may tell you that you have already made a subconscious decision.

Once you have determined the priorities of your possible tasks (budget categories in this example), you must go back to the list and determine whether you have the resources to handle all of the items or if you will have to discard or defer some. Assume that the budget allocations for the items in the previous example are as follows:

1. Food $9,000.00
2. Insurance $6,000.00
3. Gifts   Furnace   Taxes
   $3,000.00 $3,000.00 $12,000.00
4. Clothing $4,000.00
5. Tools $2,000.00
6. Computer $2,000.00
7. New Car $28,000.00

If your net available income after taxes and allowances for emergencies and home payments/maintenance (required budget items not shown in the sample allocation table) is $33,000.00, you will be able to cover only priority items one through three. In order to pay for additional listed categories, you will have to take out a loan or withdraw some savings from the bank. This means that your budget is not balanced against current income, and you will have to decide to allocate smaller amounts to the priority items or to supplement your current income by drawing upon your reserves or credit. The process is straightforward, but the results may not always come out the way you would prefer.

We have used the household budget example because it is easy to understand. It uses only money for the allocated resource. When you are considering allocations of labor and some of the other resources listed earlier, you have to analyze the availability of each resource as well as its cost. Some resources such as general labor can be expanded if you are willing to pay for them. Other resources, such as specialized expertise and time may be strictly limited, and you will have to use them wisely because you won't be able to increase them significantly. You can only improve results by becoming more efficient in use of scarce resources.

Chapter 22
Decisions Requiring Long-term Commitment

Some decisions cannot be made on a one-time basis. They require a long-term commitment. This is almost the same thing as saying that such decisions have to be made over and over again. One example of a decision requiring a long-term commitment is a decision to quit smoking. I remember hearing an unsuccessful quitter saying, "It's easy to quit smoking. I've done it a hundred times." That person had made the decision to <u>start </u>to quit many times, but he had never made a commitment to do so. Commitment requires both a decision and periodic reinforcement of that decision. In the case of cessation of smoking, the reinforcement might take the form of discussions with other quitting smokers in a support group; use of a nicotine patch, pill, or gum; or participation in hypnosis sessions. The Alcoholics Anonymous organization (AA) developed a 12-step program of commitment:

1. "We admitted we were powerless over alcohol—that our lives had become unmanageable."
2. "(We) came to believe that a Power greater than ourselves could restore us to sanity."
3. "(We) made a decision to turn our will and our lives over to the care of God *as we understand Him.*" (emphasis in original)
4. "(We) made a searching and fearless moral inventory of ourselves."
5. "(We) admitted to God, to ourselves, and to another human being the exact nature of our wrongs."
6. "(We) were entirely ready to have God remove all these defects of character."
7. "(We) humbly asked Him to remove our shortcomings."
8. "(We) made a list of all persons we had harmed, and became willing to make amends to them all."
9. "(We) made direct amends to such people whenever possible, except when to do so would injure them or others."
10. "(We) continued to take a personal inventory and when we were wrong promptly admitted it."
11. "(We) sought through prayer and meditation to improve our conscious contact with God *as we understand Him,* praying only for knowledge of His will for us and

the power to carry that out." (Emphasis in original)

12. "Having had a spiritual awakening as the result of these steps, we tried to carry this message to alcoholics, and to practice these principles." (AA, as quoted by Gary Gilley, "12-Step Recovery Programs", Biblical Discernment Ministries—12/97)

This program has been so successful that other similar groups have developed variations of it. Other organizations using 12-step commitment programs include Gamblers Anonymous, Narcotics Anonymous, Marijuana Anonymous, Cocaine Anonymous, Debtors Anonymous, National Association for Children of Alcoholics, Incest Survivors Anonymous, and Overeaters Anonymous.

Marriage is a decision for long-term commitment, and it succeeds to the extent that the many continuous interactions between the spouses reinforce the marriage vows. It is easy to pledge to love, comfort, honor, and keep each other in sickness and in health, and forsaking all others, to be faithful to each other as long as you both shall live (loosely quoted from The United Methodist Hymnal, The United Methodist Publishing House, 1989).

If it were easy to commit to these vows, we wouldn't have 50% of U.S. first marriages ending in divorce (1997 data, DivorceMagazine.com). The National Center for Health Statistics amplified this in 2001 by saying that 43 percent of first marriages break up within 15 years. Those who are truly committed to their marriages must be conscious of their determination to make it work in every spousal interaction. There are limits of conflict that should never be exceeded in any argument. The degree of comfort with each other becomes obvious through non-verbal communication habits as well as overt messages. No marital relationship is perfect, but the key ingredients to long-term success are mutual feelings of commitment and respect that support the facing of problems without allowing the development of long-term personal animosities between the spouses.

Religious conversion is another decision involving the making of a long-term commitment. Repeated participation in religious activities is the mechanism for reinforcing the conversion decision. In this case, the periodic reinforcements may be strengthened by the convert's knowledge that he or she is involved in the religious activities by choice while others may only be involved due to traditions that have been inherited.

Chapter 23
Expectations and Decisions

Davidson's Doctrine encourages you to assume that you have made a needed decision and to see whether you feel comfortable with the perceived results and implications of that assumed choice before you make the decision final. One factor that may affect your degree of comfort with the assumed decision is your level of expectations with the result. When we have low expectations, we will feel comfortable with a lower level of performance than we will if we have high expectations. For example, if we are going to purchase a used car, and we assume that we will purchase a sedan that is twelve years old for a moderate price, we will probably feel comfortable with the assumed decision if the salesperson guarantees that the car runs. However, if we assume that we will buy an expensive used sports car, our expectations for the car will be higher, and we will not feel comfortable if the only guarantee is that the car runs. Our expectations are higher, and we won't feel comfortable without more detailed and promising performance guarantees. An assumed decision that accomplishes a low-priority task does not require the same comfort level as an assumed decision that accomplishes a high priority task.

If you were on a television game show where you had to answer correctly or go home without any money, you would not have any hesitation after having answered the $100.00 question to decide to try for the $200.00 question. The consequences of an incorrect answer are not large, and you would expect the difficulty of that next question to be relatively low. However, if you had correctly answered the $50,000.00 question and had to decide whether to go on for the $100,000.00 question, you would be facing a more difficult decision. If your next answer were incorrect, you would lose the $50,000.00 that you had already won. It would be reasonable to expect the questions for larger amounts to be much more difficult than the questions for smaller amounts. Your expectations of the consequences of both failure and success become increasingly high as you proceed up the quiz show ladder of questions and prizes. Consequently, each successive decision becomes more difficult. At some point your comfort level with the next decision to ad- vance will drop to a point where you will feel more comfortable with quitting and taking the money you have already won. When that point has been reached, quitting with cash to take home is the correct decision.

Another area where varying expectations affect your decisions concerns changes of technology with time. There was a time when the idea of owning your own personal computer was unrealistic and fantastic. When personal computers first became available, technology addicts were happy to be able to purchase a computer that calculated very slowly and that they had to program themselves because there was little or no packaged software available. These results were acceptable because computer buyers had low expectations of what they could do with their own computer. Today, even the least technical computer buyer wants more computing power than once had been available to the largest scientific organizations. Our expectations have risen to the point where you virtually have to give away or discard a computer that is more than a few years old, because nobody will accept its slow calculating speed and its inability to operate with the latest software.

In professional sports teams, players were once willing to renew their contracts for a moderate percentage increase, and the negotiations took one day or less. The players' expectations were more in line with those of professionals in other conventional occupations. Today, negotiations are the province of specialized agents over a typical period of months, and a successful player will not settle until he or she receives more millions of dollars than anyone else who plays the same position. The high expectations generate increasingly high salaries for the players, but rarely lead to proportional improvements in the quality of play in their sports. Professional sports organizations have become entertainment businesses, and pay levels and ticket prices are based on how much money is received for exposing more and more people to the teams' play. The quality of play is important only in that it affects the number of people who want to watch.

Chapter 24
Making Complex Decisions

Some decisions involve very complex situations that do not allow for a single individual to act unilaterally because any choice affects the affairs of many other people. A typical complex situation that faces many people every year is planning the family gatherings at times such as Thanksgiving and Christmas. If the family has any size at all, there are married children who are torn between obligations to the two sides of the family. Multiple geographical locations may make the logistics and expense of getting together difficult. There are also obligations to give different family members a chance to host the event periodically. (The flip side of this is that no one family member should be burdened with the event every year if other family members don't want to host it.) Children in different branches of the family will have incompatible vacation schedules, and adults will have minimal travel time available. Add to this unexpected weather variations and sudden illnesses, especially among the children, and it becomes obvious that planning decisions will be difficult.

In business, you may be faced with a complex decision regarding whether or not to continue a product line that has become outdated and yields declining sales. If you keep the product line going, you will generate some income from it, but your costs will become a bigger percentage of the declining sales revenue as time passes. If you cancel the product line, you may free up resources to produce something else, but in the absence of a market for the alternate product line, you may have to make cuts in staff and facilities to reduce your costs. The situation becomes more complex if you have valued customers who depend on the old product line.

One of the best ways to handle the making of complex decisions is through an iteration process. Iterations are repeated approximations that successively lead you closer and closer to a desired result. In the case of the family gathering decision, you might arbitrarily announce the date and place of the celebration and then wait to receive objections. If none are received, you have completed the decision. If two family members have a schedule conflict, you can look for dates and places that are acceptable to those individuals, set a new tentative arrangement, and then poll the other family members for conflicts. You may find new conflicts for other family members, and you may have to repeat the procedure one or more times. Hopefully, you will find a date and place that are acceptable to all. However, if you don't find a mutually acceptable arrangement within a reasonable number of tries, you should arbitrarily select a reasonably convenient arrangement and let those family members who have remaining conflicts try to negotiate a change to their alternate situations so that they can join you. In each successive step of the planning process the key is to announce the date and place of the gathering rather than to allow each party to suggest a preference. One person has to remain in charge of the process if at all possible.

To apply the iteration process to the situation of possibly discontinuing a product line:

- Assume you have decided to continue the product line, and estimate the costs to continue the line as compared with the expected declining sales revenues.
- Assume you have decided to discontinue the product line, and estimate the continuing costs in the absence of any revenue stream.

Compare the results of the first two approaches to see which is preferable to you. At this point you will probably find that neither of these options is particularly satisfying, and you may want to consider another possibility that had not been obvious at the start of your analysis. One such possibility is:

- Assume that you have decided to increase the product price in order to get more revenue from your declining sales volume, while purchasing only enough additional short-count parts to make as many complete products as is possible with the existing parts inventory. This approach would reduce the waste of parts in inventory, would generate some additional revenue, and would give you a transition period prior to the complete shutdown of the product line. You might consider notifying your best customers of the pending shutdown in order to give them the opportunity to commit to purchasing the remaining limited product volume. They would probably be grateful for this consideration, and you would have a guarantee that you would sell your remaining products.

If you don't feel comfortable with this third possibility, you could generate another creative approach and make another iteration to your analysis. Complex decision situations usually lead to compromise solutions because there are no simple answers.

A variation on the way to handle a complex decision such as the question of whether to discontinue the obsolete product line is to divide the problem into a series of smaller decisions. This may have the advantage of making the current decision easier, but it may have the disadvantage of delaying the final choice. The easy way out of an immediate product line decision is to say nothing to the customers and to purchase just enough parts to balance up the various required parts in your inventory and delay the overall product line decision until the next time parts are needed. This buys you extra time, but it pushes you toward the decision to discontinue the line when parts are needed again. At that time the required investment in new parts will be much higher, because all the parts will be running low at approximately the same time. An interesting aspect of this type of decision situation is that each decision to continue the product line means that you will be facing the same decision in the future when parts are used up again. A decision to discontinue the line is final, but a decision to keep it in production leads to an open-ended series of decisions over a longer period of time. This may be a good thing, because no situation should continue forever without the requirement to occasionally make the deliberate commitment to continue it. The lack of such a need for recommitment is one of the key problems with many of the laws that our legislatures pass.

Chapter 25
Execution of Decisions

Once you have made any decision, you have the responsibility to execute any actions required by the decision or to have someone carry out those actions for you. If you can make a decision, but you can't bring yourself to carry it out, you have accomplished nothing. You are in the same situation as the smoker who decides to quit, but has neither the determination nor the understanding to bring his smoking habit to an end. It is really part of the decision-making process to make a plan for the steps necessary to achieve the desired result. There is really a three-step process in making any decision effective:

1. Decide.
2. Plan the steps to implement the decision.
3. Execute the steps in the plan.

Many people, especially in a complex situation or organization, think that they can make a decision and that someone else will automatically carry it out in accord with their thinking after they have made the decision. Such thinking is very naïve. First, someone else may not have the time nor be willing to take the responsibility to implement your decision. Second, persons assigned to implement a decision may not understand your detailed thinking during the process of reaching that decision. The decision-maker has to take the responsibility for implementing his/her own decision, or must generate detailed instructions for the person or persons assigned to implement it. The decision-maker must also follow up on delegated execution assignments to be sure that decisions have been implemented appropriately. If a first decision is implemented inaccurately, then a subsequent decision based upon the results of the first will also be implemented inaccurately.

Nothing is expected to be perfect, but if there is more than a small pre-agreed amount of error, you should anticipate further unacceptable errors on subsequent steps. Further, excessive errors in execution of decisions tend to be increased by subsequent implementation errors rather than to be offset by them.

In many organizations you are expected to implement your own decisions and suggestions and to petition management for the associated required funding for them. In fact, this approach is frequently used as a brake to slow down the generation of a large number of suggestions and programs in order to maintain a stable directed thrust to the organization's efforts. A decision without detailed assignment of execution responsibility may not be a decision at all, but only a "what if" speculation.

When you are assuming a decision under Davidson's Doctrine and considering its implications if that decision is actually made, one of the largest considerations will be analysis of what is required to implement it. One of the most frequent reasons for not proceeding with the decision will be an indication of extremely large cost, effort, or staffing required for you to accomplish your objective.

Chapter 26
When Decisions Make Themselves

There are many situations in which decisions make themselves. You don't have complete control over your life, and you frequently have to respond to unexpected external inputs. For example:

- A snowstorm makes it impossible for you to return home on schedule after a vacation.
- A strike by teachers makes you stay home with your children instead of going to work.
- Your doctor says you have to go to the hospital for a test.
- You receive a Jury Duty notice.
- You have to attend the funeral of a close relative.
- Your car breaks down, so you have to take the train to work.

- You get called up for military service.

The foregoing list makes it obvious that in most cases, the decisions that make themselves are usually the result of bad news, and usually involve either going someplace or not being able to go someplace. Good news, like winning the lottery, usually doesn't have the same urgency that requiring some action to be performed at a particular time. If you are an actor, you may have to go for an audition at a specific time, but when you give your performance sample you don't know whether the result will be good news or bad news. In any case, it is much easier to think of bad news situations that make your decision for you than good news situations that do the same thing.

We like to think that we have control over our actions and our decisions, and because of this, we like to plan ahead in great detail. However, sometimes things happen to negate our plans. We also have to consider our interactions with other people. Where our plans are in conflict with theirs, we may have to defer to their wishes. This is especially true for interactions with a spouse, the boss, or a policeman. Even a dog can change our immediate plans when he or she has to go out.

Most decisions that are made for you cause only brief inconveniences, but some can have a major effect on your future. Being suddenly called up for military service or having the stock market collapse when you are planning to sell stocks to make a down payment on a new house are two examples with long term implications.

The premise of this book as stated in Chapter 1 is that where you are in life is the result of all the decisions you have made or that have been made for you in the past. Each decision changes our direction somewhat. We have to be resilient enough to know that even when decisions are made for us, there will be other future choices that can at least partially compensate for them. It is also possible that some of the decisions that are made for us are beneficial in the long run. I once worked for an aerospace company that had frequent layoffs due to lost or completed contracts. Those of us who had been laid off from that company formed an "alumni association" and kept in touch over the years. In almost every case, we found that our careers had improved greatly because of the new positions, responsibilities, and education we had gained after the original layoff.

Chapter 27
Explaining Decisions and Making Excuses

Most decisions can stand on their own without explanation. However, sometimes you will make a decision that is unexpected, complicated, or controversial. In such cases you may be asked to explain your reasoning. This type of request is understandable. However, you should never make excuses for your decision. You may have had many reasons for your choice, but there is no value in defending it based on apologies and extenuating circumstances. If you have made your decision based on our principle of being able to feel comfortable with it, you should not have to make excuses. It is fine to reveal your thought process and logic in the course of deciding, but excuses are a form of insincerity and insecurity behind which people hide when they make decisions for illogical or clandestine reasons. You should be able to explain your decision if all of the contributing factors are obvious or open to examination. However, in some cases diplomacy, security, coercion, or a legal situation may make you want to avoid giving an explanation. There are also times when your decision may have been based on a hunch rather than logic. When such situations occur, simply state your decision without any explanation. Excuses will make you appear to be weak, and they will encourage people to question your motives on other occasions. When necessary maintain the appearance of being decisive but mysterious.

In the simple example of your decision to cancel an expected meeting or trip, it is better to simply say, "My plans have changed, and I won't be able to make it" than to give a story about a fictitious emergency situation. However you phrase it, you are better off giving little or no information than you are giving a false story.

If you have a business project that is running behind schedule and over the budget, don't try to appease your boss by putting blame on others or citing personality conflicts. He or she would be much better served by your indicating the unexpected extra steps which have become necessary and your plans for accomplishing them. The first approach is making excuses. The second is giving an explanation. It is important to be able to explain how you found yourself in a bad situation, but it is much more important to be able to say what you plan to do to solve that situation and move more directly from this point toward your goal. However we got here, we are here now, and we have to make the best decisions for making future progress. When you make excuses you will encourage doubt about your capabilities, and you will do nothing toward achieving your objective.

Chapter 28
When All Choices Are Good

The situation of making a decision when all choices are good is probably the most frustrating one of all. This is the proverbial "kid in a candy shop" situation. I have this problem myself. I am notorious for taking a long time deciding what to order in a restaurant where many dishes are known to be very good. Theoretically, you can't make a bad decision in such a case, but I find myself trying to optimize my choice by mentally assigning merit weights to each dish that looks interesting. This is the subjective mathematics procedure discussed in Chapter 11. For me this technique works only partially as applied to the restaurant menu. I can almost always narrow my choice down to either two or three selections. Then I have to use the deadline trick to make my final choice. I usually try to arrange to be the last one to order, and I make up my mind at ordering time.

When the waiter or waitress asks for my order I get whichever one of the two or three finalist selections that comes out of my mouth. It is an instant decision thing, and it always seems to work. When faced with a deadline, the deliberations end, and I grab a satisfactory answer. I have already narrowed down the possibilities to two or three equally acceptable options, so the last-minute selection technique always turns out to be a good one. My problem is that I thoroughly enjoy a wide variety of foods. That is why a restaurant serving a buffet or smorgasbord is always appealing to me.

Chapter 29
The Buying Decision

The stereotype is that men go shopping when they need to buy something, while women view shopping as a sport. Such generalities, while amusing, do not give a true or complete picture of our outlooks. The decision to buy something has many contributing factors. We will discuss just a few of them here.

One of the significant questions about our purchases that cuts across gender and age variations is whether we buy something because we *need* it or because we *want* it. Those who are at the lower end of the economic spectrum and those who are very practical and logical tend to buy because of need. Those who are economically well off, or those who would like others to think they are, plus those who get psychological satisfaction from making a purchase tend to purchase because of want more frequently than because of need. One of the determinants of these competing behaviors is whether you value more highly the item to be purchased or the financial ability to purchase something. Money is a form of potential energy. As long as you have it, you know that you can put it to use to purchase something. You have to decide whether it is better to spend the money now or to spend it later and gain the security that comes from having it until that time. People who are short on money tend to see security as being more important than most items or services. People who are financially free of concern about security tend to be more attracted to goods and services and may value such acquisitions as recreation and/or investments. Either way, the decision process fits with our basic assumption that you will want to make such a purchase decision based on the comfort and satisfaction that it gives you. The greatest difference between *want* and *need* purchases may be that *want* purchases are the result of subjective decisions, while *need* purchases are the result of objective decisions. If your floor is flooded because your water heater tank has burst, you have no objective choice except to buy and install a new one. If the floor is flooded because your waterbed has burst, you have more options such as buying a conventional bed instead of another waterbed, but it is still a logical and objective decision. In contrast, a decision to add a swimming pool in your back yard would probably be a subjective one.

Whenever you buy something, that item or service has both intrinsic and psychological characteristics. The intrinsic aspects are those concerned with functionality, appearance, efficiency, etc. They involve the quality of design of the item and the objective value of the service. Purchases have psychological characteristics also. Consider:

- Beauty and atmospheric qualities of a bouquet of flowers.
- Affection and friendship of a pet.
- Empowerment received from a new tool.
- Feelings of fulfillment from a vacation.
- Feelings of affection and worth involved in giving and receiving a present.

It is no accident that couples frequently try to get back to normal after an argument by giving each other gifts. A new car is like a new adventure for a family, even when it is a used vehicle that is only "new to them". A single dinner at a good restaurant or attendance at a play or sporting event can relieve long periods of stay-at-home boredom.

There is an aspect of psychological reward or tension to just about every purchase you make. The psychological dimension of a purchase can be either positive or negative. We feel positive when we purchase something we have been wanting, have needed, or which will do something good to or for us. We feel negative when we purchase something we cannot afford or which we do not want but are forced to purchase by the law or a sense of obligation. Advertising agencies craft their messages to make us think that we need rather than want the product being merchandised, and they emphasize all of its positive features in order to make us feel good about it. Manufacturers know that they need advertising to sell successfully, but there is some question as to the reason for the success of advertising. Nobel Prize winner George Stigler of the University of Chicago taught that the value of advertising is not so much due to its creativity as it is due to its function of providing information about a product or service. If this is true, then the purpose of creativity in the advertising is only to attract your attention so that you are more likely to receive the desired information.

One of the more interesting purchasing decisions occurs when you are buying something as a gift rather than for your own use. When you are purchasing something for someone else, you have to try to see the gift from their point of view in order to have a feeling for whether they would appreciate and desire it. This is very difficult, because we seldom truly understand each other. This is especially true if the beneficiary of your gift is not someone in your immediate family or someone to whom you are romantically attracted. Our lack of detailed interpersonal understanding is responsible for the large market for things that are "cute" because they appeal to surface emotions even though they may not be either wanted or needed. This is especially true during the Christmas shopping season when merchants regularly sell items that they know they couldn't sell at any other time of the year.

If you make a bad purchasing decision and end up with merchandise that is not useful to you (or if you receive a gift that is unwanted), you should not feel hesitant about returning it. It is always better to get even a partial credit or a useful exchange item than it is to have something that is useless to you taking up valuable space. Whether you are reducing storage costs or just clutter, there is economic and psychological value in eliminating useless or undesirable possessions.

Chapter 30
Investment Decisions

One of the obstacles most of us encounter with making investment decisions is the question of whether to select investments on our own or to seek professional guidance. If you choose to be self-guided in your investments, you should always favor investments in companies, funds, and financial products about which you have a large amount of information. You may obtain such information through study. Certainly, the Internet has made the search for detailed business information much easier than it was in the past. You may also discover that you are already somewhat of an expert with regard to the industry in which you work if you have been regularly following technical and business developments in your trade magazines. If you choose to seek professional advice, you should be very cautious about relying on advice from someone who has a conflict of interest in that he or she has a financial stake in the investment being recommended. It is also not always easy to determine the qualifications of someone who is presented as an investment professional. As in the case with medical decisions, it is to your advantage to obtain as many independent reliable opinions as possible about a proposed investment and the person who is offering it.

I am not qualified to give anyone specific investment advice, but several generalities about investing may be useful:

- Every dollar you earn gives you an amount of "economic potential energy". As long as you hold that dollar, you have a dollar's worth of that potential. The dollar does not become actualized value until you trade it for something else. Whether you trade it for goods, services, or an investment, the dollar's potential value goes to zero after it has been spent. The item upon which you spend the dollar may have its own potential value as far as future resale or exchange, but the dollar is no longer in your hands, and thus no longer has potential value.

- That dollar you hold also has a time dimension. You can spend it or save it. If you spend it, the dollar is gone. If you save it, you may choose to use it for investment purposes. If you invest the dollar, its value may rise or fall, depending on whether you have a positive or negative return on your investment. The value may increase or decrease if you have invested in something like stock that is traded on a market. Most people think that bank accounts being federally insured can only increase in value. However, you must look at the interest rate and fee structure of the bank to see whether your dollar in the bank is growing faster, net of fees, than its long-term decrease due to continuing inflation.

- One of the problems with investing in this age of high speed information transfer is that by the time you, as a market outsider, receive news that the market or your stock is moving rapidly higher (or lower), it has already happened. In almost every case, you will miss the point of rapid upward or downward acceleration and will have to settle for participating in the after-shocks and adjustments of the market. For this reason the traditional Wall Street adages are "Sell on good news." and "Buy on bad news." If you consistently manage to act counter to the market *in a knowledgeable way*, you will end up selling at a high price and buying at a low price more frequently than not. The hard part is learning enough to understand the stock and the nature of the market sufficiently to actually accomplish this market-contrary behavior in a profitable way.

- Because of the difficulty in achieving profitable market-contrary behavior, many experts say that the average investor is better off making regularly spaced investments in the stock market or a mutual fund *whether the market is moving upward or downward,* and then holding those investments for the long term. This approach has some tax and fee benefits over frequent buying and selling, but it leaves you open to occasional setbacks like the Enron bankruptcy that hurt many investors.

Very few investors have the time or the expertise to gather all of the appropriate information, find truly expert assistance, and make the proper buying and selling decisions to be consistently successful in investing. That is why mutual funds are so popular and why you should only invest cash that is not required to offset current needs and possible short-term emergencies. In this latter regard, you are usually better off investing in a liquid asset which can be converted back to cash easily, such as a stock or bank account, than a fixed asset, such as a house or factory, that may be difficult to sell if you need cash quickly.

You have to analyze your own situation in detail to determine whether you already have enough liquidity to offset the foregoing suggestion in favor of investing in the long-term real estate upward trend. You should also consider whether you are comfortable with investing in only one or a few assets as opposed to spreading your risk by investing in many different stocks or other assets.

Chapter 31
Impacting Political and Government Decisions

Whether you are an elected official, an employee of a government agency, a concerned voter, or a student, you are affected by the decisions made by government bodies and by the way they reach those decisions. You have at one time or another probably been concerned about the possibility of influencing those decisions. Government decisions assist us, or they set limits on our future possibilities. They free us of retirement worries, or they put limits on our pensions. They encourage us toward lifelong learning, or they give us fears for the future. You have to pay attention to them.

One of the characteristics of government in the United States and most developed countries is that there are many levels of government. While you may never deal directly with the President, you will undoubtedly have direct dealings with government bodies and agencies at some level. When questioned, most government representatives will say that their job is to serve the people. Your job is to see that they do serve you.

One of the most important things you should keep in mind when you are attempting to get some attention from elected officials is that they probably want to get reelected at the end of their current term. Because of this, you will always receive more attention from such an official if you ask for his or her assistance as a member of a group rather than as an individual. Groups have more votes than individuals. You may be approaching the official as an individual, but give the <u>impression</u> of group representation. Several ways of doing this include:

- If this is a local matter, say that "our neighborhood" would like...or that you have been polling people living in your area and the overwhelming majority of them have said that...
- When writing a letter use business or peer group or church letterhead when possible, but do not specifically say that you are speaking for that organization unless it is the truth and sanctioned by them.
- Be a "name dropper" and indicate that someone who has political influence or who represents a large group suggested that you contact this official for action on your problem.

- In this age of the Internet, you can even create your own group web site or blog so that you actually do represent a checkable point of view.

There are some situations when you are trying to get satisfaction or personal attention from a bureaucratic agency rather than from a single elected official. In such instances you will want to follow a strategy that will make your case appear important enough to cause very busy office workers to interrupt their routines and give you high priority.

- Many years ago, when I had inadvertently missed a deposit/report deadline for my business with the IRS, that agency said that a sizeable fine was due. Instead of arguing with the IRS I wrote a letter on company letterhead to my Senator. I complained to him that IRS fines were out of proportion to the amount of tax involved for small businesses and that fines should not be levied when there is a long history of prompt payment. I received a very nice letter back from the Senator (Adlai Stevenson III from Illinois) saying that he agreed with my arguments and would contact the IRS on my behalf. Within a week the IRS sent me a notice that the fine had been cancelled. Whether you are talking about a government agency or a large business, intervention from a person higher in the organization will get the attention of a bureaucrat very quickly.

- If you cannot find someone higher in the chain of command that will intervene on your behalf, use the name of such a person who declined your request, and go to the agency yourself. Simply say, "I was discussing this problem with the Mayor (or other official to whom you had actually appealed) and she directed me to you as the person who would be able to resolve the issue." The statement is true, but you may have changed the emphasis in the Mayor's instructions for you to take care of it yourself.

- When all else fails, if you have a problem that occurs for many people, and you cannot get satisfaction from a bureaucratic government agency, refer that problem to your local TV news organization. TV news people get immediate attention from government agencies because of the potential for bad publicity if they are ignored. The news people also realize that they get extra viewers and a very good reputation if they show that they investigate government wrongdoing on behalf of the people.

Good government officials realize that the legitimacy of their positions comes from being responsive to the needs of the people who elected them and whom they are paid to serve. They want to show leadership and commitment to their values, but they tend to get overwhelmed with the many day-to-day details of their jobs. As is the case for many in business, they have so much to do that it is difficult to accomplish anything important. If you have need of assistance from government at any level, you will get that assistance if you make your matter appear to be very important, or if you make your request appear to be so easy to satisfy that it won't interfere with other competing projects. It may also help if make sure that the official knows that he or she will get public credit for a satisfactory conclusion and public blame for an unsatisfactory one. When you want an official to decide to help you, your task is to make that official see that decision as very easy, logical, and potentially rewarding.

Chapter 32
When Other People Make Decisions for You

There are many times when your life is shaped by decisions that other people make for you. The majority of these decisions are made when you are a child and your parents or guardians speak for you in the eyes of society. As you grow older, school and college authorities, military officers, and legislators will make a wide assortment of decisions for you. Your spouse will impose more than a few decisions on you, although hopefully you will contribute input for most spousal decisions. Doctors will impose decisions on you with regard to health matters. When you get to be a senior citizen you may find yourself in an assisted living situation where the administrators dictate most aspects of everyday living.

My mother, like many other parents, told me when I was a child that I could grow up to be President of the United States. I am continually grateful that she was wrong on that one. I can't think of a more burdensome or more thankless job, especially in this age when so many people of each party think that anyone who disagrees with their political views is evil.

There was a time when people were willing to respect differences of opinion. I remember when, during the 1956 presidential contest between Dwight Eisenhower and Adlai Stevenson, my mother decided to hold an election night party. She sent me out to both political headquarters to get campaign buttons and posters. She invited guests without knowing their political leanings, and as they arrived they could put on their preferred campaign button if they desired. It was a pleasant event for all. Those were the days when results were announced gradually over a period of several hours rather than having networks predict winners prematurely. Because of this everyone at the party enjoyed cheering for his or her candidate as the periodic updates to the tallies were revealed on TV.

As you grow from a youth to a young adult, there will be times when parents and other authority figures will continue to want to make a decision for you, but when you will feel that you should make it on your own. One of the key determinants of your maturity will be when you are ready to face an important decision and say that you want to make it on your own because if the decision is wrong, you are the one who will bear the consequences. You should feel that you would rather bear consequences resulting from your own decisions rather than due to the decisions of others.

We like to think that we have the freedom to make all of our own choices. However, we also have to learn how to cope with the decisions that external authorities make for us. For some people this is difficult, but if there were a complete absence of rules and regulations that affect all of us society would turn into anarchy. If this were to happen, you would no longer be free to decide to choose a career or a life style in the confidence that you would be left alone to pursue it so long as your choice didn't harm others.

We have to realize that we don't make decisions in isolation. Every decision has a context. While we want to be free to make our own decisions, we have to understand that our decisions affect others, and perhaps limit their freedom to make their own choices. Anyone who can make decisions that affect someone else has a degree of power over that person. We have to be careful as we exercise such power if we want to be good citizens and friends. We make better choices when we consider during the decision-making process whether we are adversely affecting someone else by our actions. We become part of their context, and they become part of ours. They may respond to our decision affecting them by making one or more decisions that affect us as well as others. We have to conclude that even when others are not making decisions for us, they are making decisions that in some way affect us and which may influence our future actions.

Chapter 33
Decisions You Would Rather Not Make

Many times during your life you will be faced with a decision that you wish you didn't have to make. You may have great difficulty in making such decisions, but you usually know that they have to be made and that you are the only one that can make them. Typically, it is less a question of selecting the proper choice from among several alternatives than it is a choice that you know is the correct one, but you just don't want to implement it.

One especially difficult situation of this type is the life or death decision. You may have to say goodbye to a pet that has been an integral part of your family for many years. You may know that old age and failing health make it difficult for the animal to get through each day, but you want to put off the decision for as long as possible. You can stall your decision for a certain amount of time, but you know in your heart that it will have to be made sooner rather than later. No one can tell you what to do in this situation. It is one of the unpleasant moments that are part of life. I have faced this situation several times, and the only affirming comment I can contribute is that when you lose a pet at the end of its life, you may become open to giving another animal the chance to enter your home and your heart.

The situation is, of course, much more difficult when you are facing the probable end of life of a person who is close to you. You will seldom be put in the pet-related situation of having to decide the timing of a person's death, but the implications of that pending event will be ever so much greater in the case of a person.

One of the underlying reasons we feel so bothered by the death or pending death of someone who has been connected to us in any way, is that such an event makes us feel a bit closer to our own eventual passing. Most people try to live life on a day-by-day basis without thinking about its eventual end, because life is more enjoyable that way, and we have little control over the end anyway. As suggested in the Irish saying in Chapter 4, "Why worry?"

Beyond life and death decisions, there are many other choices we try to avoid. In some cases we feel that people will think less of us if we make a required decision. In such instances, we should remember that it is less important to think of how people will react to our decision than how we will rate ourselves for having made it. If you know that it is the right thing to do, the decision should be the focus of your actions and not other people's feelings toward you.

If we have a phobia or a strong fear or distaste for something, we will do everything possible to avoid it, even if someone suggests that facing the fear will help us to overcome it. Most of us have something that bothers us psychologically, and even if we feel that discomfort is irrational, we feel much more comfortable if we avoid it. It is always easier to go around your personal barrier than it is to go through or over it. This approach works well so long as avoiding your fear affects nobody else significantly. However, you may have to choose to face your problem in an emergency situation. For instance, if you have an extremely sick relative or friend, and you are afraid to fly, you may have to face flying in order to reach that person in a timely manner. Usually, an emergency will make phobias much easier to overcome. I strongly doubt that there are many parents who would not overcome their fear of water in order to try to save their drowning child.

Another type of decision we would rather not make involves a situation where every option will hurt someone. This might occur when a couple is considering the breakup of their marriage and its effects on their young children. If they separate or get divorced, it will lead to traumatic times and decisions for the children. If they stay together to simplify life for the children, the parents will have continuing problems with each other plus ambiguities in explaining their situation to the children.

A similarly all-choices-are-bad situation occurs when a company has to face closing because of bad economic conditions. Is it better to lay off employees in order to reduce huge losses or to seek additional loans at the risk of even larger future losses? This company situation is probably easier to handle than that of the family with problems because money is a more objective criterion than are emotions, and because there are probably some creative options for resolving the company difficulties that have no parallel in the family context. For instance, the company could attempt to reduce hours, renegotiate wages, or "lease out" employees in order to reduce costs without reducing staff. They could also try to cut back on facilities and outside services instead of staff people.

Some decisions that you would rather not make are those that would leave you with a feeling of guilt. Mothers have always been experts at swaying your choices in these cases. For instance, an adult child might be considering taking a job in a different part of the country, in the face of his or her mother saying, "Go ahead; take the job. Don't worry about me back here all by myself. I'll get along." Similarly, it is difficult to decide to be out of town for a business event that conflicts with the timing of an important event for your child. A supervisor at work may tell you that you don't have to take an unwanted assignment with the implication that you will be considered disloyal if you don't. All of these examples use the feeling of guilt to pressure you into accepting a preferred behavior. You have to decide whether the contrary behavior is important enough to you for you to accept that guilt.

There can be creative variations on the guilt technique of influencing people. Take the example cited above of the mother's reaction to a child considering a job out of town. When my sister and brother-in-law were considering just such a move from the East Coast to the West Coast, they told my mother, and her reaction was to say that she was ready to move with them. Their response was to decide not to make the move after all.

Chapter 34
End of Life Decisions

Decisions regarding the end of your life should be made well in advance of that point. If you put them off too long, you may not be in suitable physical or mental condition to make them wisely. You should discuss your desires with your family and have an attorney with experience in such issues and with no financial interest in your estate set your wishes onto paper. Typical issues to plan in advance are:

- A Will describing how your assets are to be distributed.
- Desired arrangements for your funeral and your choice of burial or cremation.
- Organ donation desires if applicable.
- A Living Will indicating in advance your desires with regard to efforts to keep you alive in extreme illness if you are unable

to give your informed consent at that time.

- Selection of the Executor of your Will.
- Designation of someone with Power of Attorney for financial matters in the event that you are not capable of making financial decisions.
- Designation of someone with Power of Attorney for health matters in the event that you are not capable of making health decisions.

In addition, you should plan to periodically prepare and/or update a physical and financial inventory of your assets to clarify what your Will covers and where all of the assets are located. You should record a listing of all of your passwords and their uses for all computer-based transactions. You should update your Will whenever there is a change in family situation (e.g., new children, marriages, divorces, or deaths) so that there is no ambiguity about your wishes and so that no one is inadvertently omitted. You may also want to contact a tax expert about planning your financial affairs in order to minimize taxes on your estate and taxes to your heirs.

Nobody likes to dwell on considerations regarding death, but proper advance planning will actually make life easier. Planning may remove the burden of making arrangements during the final stage of your life. At that time you may be under considerable stress and may not want to make important decisions. Early planning may also prevent other people from making decisions that are in conflict with your wishes when you are not in complete control of the situation.

Chapter 35
Good/Better/Best Decisions

If you have absorbed the contents of this book, you will hopefully be aware of the importance of decision-making to the journey you make through life. The principles that we have discussed should help you to make decisions with which you will be able to feel comfortable. As such, your decisions will be good decisions for you. This is a personal matter. A decision that is good for you may not be one that would be good for me. We all travel different roads through life, and who is to say which one is the best? If you are comfortable with your decision and its outcome, and if you are willing to re-evaluate your decisions and make new ones as needed for continued personal comfort, you are deciding well. There is no one best path for you as directed by your decisions and those that are made for you by others. Be satisfied if you feel you have made good decisions. Re-evaluate ones with which you have not felt comfortable until they become good decisions. A good decision is just as good as a "better" decision and just as good as a "best" decision because no one can tell them apart. The grass is *not* always greener on the other side of the fence. You are the only one who can evaluate your personal comfort with an assumed subjective decision. Have the courage to do that evaluation, and then make that assumed choice real. The process becomes more and more automatic as it is repeated. Choices are not things to be delayed without good reason. Decision Time is now!

ABOUT THE AUTHOR

Richard Davidson is the author of the self-help guidebook: *DECISION TIME! Better Decisions for a Better Life*. He has written the five-novel Lord's Prayer Mystery Series: *Lead Us Not into Temptation*, *Give Us this Day our Daily Bread*, *Forgive Us Our Trespasses*, *Thy Will Be Done*, and *Deliver Us from Evil*. He has edited an anthology, *Overcoming: An Anthology by the Writers of* OCWW. His latest three novels, *Implications, Impulses,* and *Impostor* from his new Imp Mysteries series, continue to chronicle the exploits of Arthur Blake and the investigative associates who aided him in the earlier mystery series, taking their interests in new directions. Mr. Davidson is Past President of Off-Campus Writers' Workshop, the oldest ongoing group of its kind in the U.S. and is the founder of the ReadWorthy Books Book Review Blog. He is the founder of the Independent Mystery Publishing Society (IMPS). Mr. Davidson is a Certified Lay Servant Speaker and a former Lay Leader in the United Methodist Church. He is also an aeronautical & astronautical engineer and a businessman.

WORKS BY THIS AUTHOR

NONFICTION:

DECISION TIME! Better Decisions for a Better Life,
Second Edition
RADMAR Publishing
ISBN 978-0-9829160-7-0 (paperback)
ISBN 978-1-4581-8395-8 (Smashwords eBook)
ASIN B0052GOZEO (Kindle Edition eBook)

Where you are in life today is the result of all of the past decisions you have made or which have been made for you in response to the various situations and events that have impacted your life. The decisions that you will make from this point forward will determine the degree to which your future will be positive or negative. *DECISION TIME!* gives you insight into the subjective decision-making process as applied to both small and large choices you will face. It includes dynamic aspects, cultural effects, and morality as applied to decision-making for individuals, teams, corporations, and societies. *DECISION TIME!* prepares you to face the continuous impacts of decision situations confidently and without hesitation.

FICTION:

Lead Us Not into Temptation (The Lord's Prayer Mystery Series, Volume I),
Second Edition
RADMAR Publishing
ISBN 978-0-9976381-0-3 (paperback)
ISBN 978-1-4581-7381-2 (Smashwords eBook)
ASIN B01GEK7ZZ2 (Kindle Edition eBook)

Arthur Blake, former NASA engineer turned minister, receives an emergency appointment to be pastor of the United Methodist Church in Parkville, a distant suburb of Chicago, following the bizarre sudden death of the church's unusual former pastor. Pastor Blake's attempts to unravel the mystery that shrouds his predecessor become involved with tracking the child of a possibly bigamous soldier in World War II England, art and jewelry treasures plundered by the Nazis and their sympathizers, and the eventual results of childhood sibling conflicts in combined families. Arthur's allies in his investigation include Parkville Police Chief Bobby Andrews, County Medical Examiner Irma Custis, and the married team of Penny and Joe Gonzalez who work for a clandestine government agency. During the course of *Lead Us Not into Temptation*, the reader discovers how seemingly minor historical events lead to major present-day dislocations in church, village, and family relationships.

Give Us this Day Our Daily Bread (The Lord's Prayer Mystery Series, Volume II)
Second Edition
RADMAR Publishing
ISBN 978-0-9829160-5-6 (paperback)
ISBN 978-1-4580-6717-3 (Smashwords eBook)
ASIN B01H7M47M0 (Kindle Edition eBook)

Arthur Blake, Pastor of Parkville United Methodist Church, has to deal with the aftereffects of a traumatic communion incident. He works to assist the authorities in investigating the cause while doing his best to convince members of his congregation that it is safe to return to church. Working with the police and federal agencies, he discovers that the terror of the initial event is minor compared with the potential chaotic impact of future disasters being planned by the perpetrator. The investigation is interwoven with several relationship situations that affect the final outcome.

Forgive Us Our Trespasses (The Lord's Prayer Mystery Series, Volume III)
Second Edition
RADMAR Publishing
ISBN 978-0-9976381-1-0 (paperback)
ISBN 978-1-4657-3739-7 (Smashwords eBook)
ASIN B005SULQ6Y (Kindle Edition eBook)

Arthur Blake, Pastor of Parkville United Methodist Church, tries to assist his father to resolve his trauma after learning that his best friend, recently killed in a car accident, may have been an imposter with a heinous background. The investigation reveals that the presumed accident was but one link in a chain of murders. Blake works to determine the true identity of his father's friend, while also discovering the man's past activities and affiliations. Arthur works to solve the murders in conjunction with his colleagues at ABC Consultants. He also draws on assistance from associates at a covert government agency with which he has worked before. The coordinated effort to solve the puzzle examines incidents that span the period between World War II and the present in order to defuse the personal, national, and international dangers resulting from them.

Thy Will Be Done (The Lord's Prayer Mystery Series, Volume IV)
RADMAR Publishing
ISBN 978-0-9829160-2-5 (paperback)
ISBN 978-1-3013-4293-8 (Smashwords eBook)
ASIN B009JU6EZM (Kindle Edition eBook)

The sudden death of a young woman attending Parkville United Methodist Church infuriates her brother and leads to congregational outrage over his outburst and subsequent murder. The investigation of that slaying by Pastor Arthur Blake and his associates leads to revelations of a previously undetected criminal organization operating in the area. Unraveling the mystery and scope of this group entangles Arthur and his associated investigators in a web of conspiracies extending from Illinois to both U.S. coasts and through Mexico to Guatemala.

Deliver Us from Evil (The Lord's Prayer Mystery Series, Volume V)
RADMAR Publishing
ISBN 978-0-9829160-3-2 (paperback)
ASIN: B00EBDUXFY (Kindle Edition eBook)

Arthur and Irma's wedding day has finally arrived, but an unexpected interruption leads to their need to investigate a possible murder committed by someone close to them. With the aid of friends and federal agents Penny and Joe Gonzalez, they follow a series of clues, crisscrossing the United States to learn more about the murder, related subsequent events, and the significance of a rare object brought home by a veteran of the Iraq War. A second murder close to Pastor Arthur Blake's church involves them in a new investigation, assisting Parkville Police Chief Bobby Andrews. Are these murders and the tracking of that strange object connected? Will marriage deteriorate or improve the relationship between Arthur and Irma? Character flaws in many relationships color the outcome.

Overcoming: An Anthology by the Writers of OCWW
Edited and with an Introduction by Richard Davidson
RADMAR Publishing
ISBN 978-9829160-4-9 (paperback)
ASIN B00E80NN4I (Kindle Edition eBook)

This anthology covers many aspects of overcoming life's problems, obstacles, and challenging developments. The contributing writers have used fiction, non-fiction, memoir, poetry, historical chronicle, and drama to highlight our continuing need to overcome our problems, rather than dwell on them. The reader will learn from many talented writers the skills needed to respond constructively, energetically, and sometimes humorously to whatever obstacle bars one's path. Apply their lessons to your own needs and to those of others you cherish.

Implications: An Arthur Blake Mystery Novel
RADMAR Publishing
ISBN 978-0-9829160-6-3 (paperback)
ASIN B00LY9IBWK (Kindle Edition eBook)

Bishop Howard Chandler has assigned Pastor Arthur Blake to investigate the burning of a church in the small city of Amboy, Illinois. He learns from that church's pastor that she had to overcome past improprieties by former members. During the investigation of the fire's cause, Arthur and the other state fire investigators uncover disturbing aspects of the ninety-year-old church's design and history. Arthur calls on his federal associates for assistance, as the investigation of a local church fire expands to seeking solutions to related crimes occurring from the present to recent years and back to the Prohibition Era. Progress in the investigation intertwines with new developments in Arthur's family life.

Impulses: An Arthur Blake Mystery Novel (Imp Mysteries, Volume 2)
RADMAR Publishing
ISBN 978-0-9829160-8-7 (paperback)
ASIN B012LFQXYI (Kindle Edition eBook)

Several disturbing dreams cause Arthur Blake to wonder whether he is trying to do too much for the many people who seek his services. These qualms are complicated by Bishop Howard Chandler's suggestion that Arthur temporarily set aside his official duties and take an extended sabbatical leave. His resulting internal debates about career moves are set aside when the pastor who replaced him at the Parkville church dies in an apparent suicide possibly linked to several deaths at the Parkville Rehabilitation Home. The bishop assigns Arthur to determine the circumstances behind the new pastor's death, while Arthur and Irma, his wife and constant investigative partner, also study a mysterious shipment at his father's antiques shop. The sudden disappearance of a young associate provides another mystery and leads to questions of life after death and reincarnation. Events that initially appear simple become increasingly complex as the true natures of many people come into question.

Impostor: A Genealogical Mystery (Imp Mysteries, Volume 3)
RADMAR Publishing
ISBN 978-0-9829160-9-4

When Debbie Danforth discovers a flaw in the genealogy of her live-in boyfriend, Jeremy Hadley, he and his family try to discredit her findings, but eventually admit they must be true. Jeremy and Debbie run a private detective business, the Sandley Agency and commit their skills and resources to learning about the impostor Debbie has discovered in the Hadley ancestry. They are assisted in this effort by Penny and Joe Gonzalez, principals in a covert federal agency, with whom Jeremy has previously worked as a consultant. Their joint investigation uncovers both unique details concerning the mysterious Hadley impostor and little-known facts about events leading up to World War II in both Britain and the United States. Was the person who masqueraded as a Hadley a villain or a hero? Did other Hadleys know he was a fraudulent member of their family? Did his actions assist or impede the British and the Americans as they faced the growing menace in prewar Europe?

Learn more about the writings, humor, and random thoughts of Richard Davidson at: radmarinc.com davidsonbookshelf.com betterlifedecisions.blogspot.com and at the Independent Mystery Publishing Society (IMPS) https://www.mysteryimps.com
Richard Davidson's author page on Amazon is located at https://www.amazon.com/author/richarddavidson Follow and *Like* Richard Davidson, Author on Facebook at https://www.facebook.com/richarddavidsonauthor?ref=hl
Follow him on Twitter @mysteryimp

www.ingramcontent.com/pod-product-compliance
Lightning Source LLC
Chambersburg PA
CBHW052002090426
42741CB00008B/1515